Prophecy *Unleashed* is a phenomenal prophetic testament of just how God divinely intervenes in our lives even when we aren't completely aware of what life truly entails. It is an anointed, yoke-destroying, chain breaking and authentic read that will strengthen any believer to walk in purpose, to answer the call upon their life and understand the gifts that God has bestowed upon them.

Instructed by the voice of God, Prophetess Natisha Wilson brings to light how God can take what others consider as ordinary and transform it into extraordinary. It is evident with each chapter that Prophetess Wilson was ushered by the power of God as she penned each word under the unction of the Holy Ghost. Through her undaunted anointing she reveals through prophetic insight how God is divinely positioning His people for the latter rain and abundant overflow by the Word of Truth.

Prophecy *Unleashed* speaks not only to the believer but also to the broken-hearted, to the dreamer, to the hurting and even to the anointed. As you read each sentence, Prophetess Wilson challenges the reader to tentatively listen to the voice of God and allow Him to minister to the heart. Stepping outside the box, **Prophecy *Unleashed*** is a candid and uncut revelation of the intimate relationship God desires from His people and how we must operate in kingdom authority.

Prophecy *Unleashed* declares to the reader we are no longer bound by excuses. God is breaking down all the barriers and propelling us from the background to the forefront. Now is our time! God has mapped out our very steps. Purpose was birthed in you for this very moment. You have a champion within you, now *unleash it!*

Prophecy
Unleashed

Prophetess Natisha E. Wilson

Prophecy Unleashed

By: Prophetess Natisha E. Wilson

ISBN: 987-1-57550-088-1

First Edition

Published by: Natisha E. Wilson

Cover Design: CTS Graphics

Dedication

This book is dedicated to my husband
Elder Jason Wilson, Sr.
You have stood with me through it all from day one.
Your love and selflessness is God-given and
I know I am truly a blessed woman of God.

To my children Julia, Natalie, and Jase
thanks for being mommy's little helpers.
You three give me the love that keeps me going.

Acknowledgements

To my family, I am without words. Thank you for all your love and support. You have encouraged me to keep pressing forward…to not give up on the process.

To my best friend, you know who you are. What's understood doesn't need explaining. I love you and thanks for being you.

To my church family, Lighthouse Apostolic Ministries of God Church, my prayer is that God continue to keep you and bless you for allowing me to operate freely in my gift.

Contents:

Preface

We pray expecting God to answer. We say speak Lord, expecting God to speak. We cry out use me Lord…not truly knowing how and when God will use us. But we must be ready to be used. For the Bible says in Matthew 24:44, "*Therefore be ye also ready…*" So, I prayed. I cried even unto our God, use me Lord. But I wasn't ready. I never imagined that God would pour out this anointing, this gift on me to prophesy.

Prophecy; [1]the foretelling or prediction of what is to come. [2] something that is declared by a prophet, especially a divinely inspired prediction, instruction or exhortation [3] a divinely inspired utterance or revelation.

-Dictionary.com

Introduction

Nineteen years and counting, I have served God with my whole heart starting as a child and even to this day. I can say my heart has changed. Change you may say? Ah, but yes, change it has. For this gift of prophecy has caused me to love God the more, not just for the gift; but for the call.

You don't have to run. There's no need to be afraid. Embrace who God has called you to be; even if that means walking into the unknown. I know it may not be easy and believe me I do know. It takes faith to walk this Christian journey.

'For we walk by faith, not by sight.' (2 Corinthians 5:7)

It takes dying to self and being sensitive to the voice of God. I accept who I am. I didn't always know, but today I know who I am and whose I am. Even more so, God knows who I am.

'Before I formed thee in the belly I knew thee; and before thou camest forth out of the womb I sanctified thee and I ordained thee a prophet unto the nations.' (Jeremiah 1:5)

Sanctified…that I am. Ordained of God? Yes, I am before the foundations of the world. I will not restrain this gift anymore. I can no longer ignore the call upon my life. I welcome the call. Here I am Lord! I embrace it and I unleash it.

Chapter 1: In the Beginning

It all started in the beginning; when prophecy unleashed itself. It took me by storm April 11, 1999 on a Sunday. This is a day that was always designed as a part of my destiny. It was only a small storefront church in the inner city of St. Louis on the corner of DeSoto and West Florissant. My granny brought my sister and me and several of our cousins to church with her. We had attended other churches with her in the past, but this church and this day would set the stage for the rest of my life. I sat through the singing, preaching, and the pastor's wife did the altar call. She asked if anyone wanted to be saved. She recited the plan of salvation and the invitation was made. I can't tell you just how I got up the courage to go up to the altar but that's where I was, giving my life to Christ.

I still can recall the damp tarry room and musty basement used for baptisms; it's here that I received the Holy Ghost with the evidence of speaking in tongues.

> *'Then Peter said unto them, Repent, and be baptized every one of you in the name of Jesus Christ for the remission of sins, and ye shall receive the gift of the Holy Ghost.'* (Acts 2:38)

Once I received the Holy Ghost it was certain that I now needed to be baptized. The pastor took my sister and me downstairs in the basement and the saints began to sing, 'I'm going down in Jesus' name.' My granny was in the corner praising God. I was filled with emotion. I was scared but I was excited too. All I knew was I wanted more of God.

I was baptized in Jesus' name in a makeshift baptism pool. It was a horse trough filled with cold icy water. When I came up, the saints were still singing but this time they sang, 'I've **been** down in Jesus' name.' I was now a candidate for Heaven. I was now born again.

I was only 16 years old when I was saved. It's funny that even then, you think you know just how your life would go. You have your whole life mapped out. You know where you're going to go, what you're going to do, who you are going to become. My plans: first graduate high school, go to college, and then grad school; get married and have kids. Boy, was I wrong. God had different plans in store for my life. He knew the path I would take. He ordered my very steps. I didn't realize at the time that my life was not my own. This was only the beginning.

'*¹⁹What? Know ye not that your body is the temple of the Holy Ghost which is in you, which ye have of God, and ye are not your own? ²⁰ For ye are bought with a price: therefore glorify God in your body, and in your spirit, which are God's.*' (2 Corinthians 6:19-20)

We went to church with my granny every Sunday. I was in awe of the presence of God. The way the Spirit moved throughout the sanctuary amazed me. It took my very breath away. I had never seen anything so beautiful. The saints were singing, clapping, speaking in tongues, and praising God. I can still hear the jingle of the tambourines, the rhythm of the drums, and the melody of the organ. I wanted that. I wanted to be like the older saints. I always longed for God even as a child.

In the sixth grade, I remember I did not fully understand who God is, so I picked up the phone and called to schedule for Mormons to come to our home. The TV commercial said if you wanted to know more about the life of Jesus Christ, pick up the phone and call. Call I did. My mother was a single parent at the time. It was just her, my sister, and me living in a two-bedroom apartment. There was a knock on the door. I completely forgot I called them a week before. My mother had to sit and listen to their perspective of holiness. They gave me what I thought was 'The Other Bible' and left. My mom was not pleased … to say the least.

Nonetheless, can't you see I wanted to know God. I wanted to know His ways. I wanted to feel His glory. I wanted to learn of Him. My heart searched for the deep places of God. I was drawn to Him like a moth to a flame.

'¹O God, thou art my God; early will I seek thee: my soul thirsteth for thee, my flesh longeth for thee in a dry and thirsty land, where no water is; ²To see thy power and thy glory, so as I have seen thee in the sanctuary, ³Because thy loving kindness is better than life, my lips shall praise thee...' (Psalms 63: 1-3)

It's something unexplainable about God. When you are called to Him He knows how to get your attention. He had my attention as far back as I can remember. Down memory lane, I can now see the handprints of God all over my life. Wow! My God! My God! How could I not know it was Him? I was always curious. I just needed to know this thing called life. I just needed to know the one they called God. I could always hear a small voice with me everywhere I went...a presence that seemed to follow me as a child. Now I know you're saying, 'that's just an imaginary friend. All kids have them.' Yes and no. Yes, most kids do have them. But no, this wasn't that. Now that I am older, I know God had revealed Himself to me. It's apparent. No dispute. Hands down. It was God!

The older I became, the voice was comforting and the presence reassuring. He was my friend first before I knew Him as God. When you grow up always being picked last, always looked over, often alone, sometimes a friend is all you need.

'A man that hath friends must shew himself friendly: and there is a friend that sticketh closer than a broth-

er.' (Proverbs 18:24)

What a friend I have in Jesus!

As early as I can remember I began writing to my friend. You may know Him. Some call Him Jehovah. Some call Him Yahweh. I call him Jesus! It was easy to tell my secrets, to share my day, to unveil the hidden things in my heart. Before I knew it, I filled journal after journal with letters to God. Even today, nothing has changed. I had to be in sixth grade then and I had the ultimate best friend ever. Like old friends chatting, it started with me doing all the talking or should I say all the writing? Without warning, that small still voice became louder. Attention please! God is speaking!

So often I assumed that the visions and the dreams were deja'vu. I didn't understand then. My parents weren't saved. Who could I go to? Who could I share these things with and not sound crazy? Just like a puzzle that I could not piece together, was the fact that God was truly showing me things in the spirit. So, I just kept writing…not even knowing God was preparing me for what was to come.

Fast forward four years: a sixteen-year-old sophomore in high school, filled with the Holy Ghost wasn't always a walk in the park. I always was a loner. I never had many friends. However, that didn't matter at the moment. I wanted to tell everybody my good news. I told my best friend at the time. I told anybody who would listen. How could I explain it? I never felt this way before. It was like I could see the world crystal clear. It was if the scales had fallen from my eyes. I felt the weight of the world was off my shoulders.

At sixteen years old I felt out of tune with life. I was a very shy teenager. Being overweight, I didn't have much luck with the boys. Even then I always longed to be loved for me. Don't get me wrong, my mother always hugged and kissed my sister and me every day. It was instilled in us to love and to forgive at a young age. We were raised to never let a day go by without saying, 'I love you.' Even still, I longed for love. You have to understand, I struggled with low self-esteem then. It's bizarre. The very thing I longed for, had been searching for, was in God all the time.

'For God so loved the world that he gave his only be-gotten Son, that whosoever believeth in him should not perish, but have everlasting life.' (John 3:16)

I embraced the changes. It sounds weird saying it out loud now but before I got saved, I struggled practicing sin. I didn't drink alcohol. I never smoked. I wasn't sexually active. I couldn't even swear like the other kids. I didn't go to parties. In fact, some of my peers called me Mama Tish. Man, oh man, the devil had me deceived. I thought I was a good person. I thought all the good I've done would grant me wings like an angel. I thought God would see my good deeds and write my name in the Book. I thought my 'goodness' would guarantee my spot in Heaven. This could not be further from the truth.

'For there is not a just man upon this earth, that doeth good and sinneth not.' (Ecclesiastes 7:20)

I thank God for saving me from sin; even from myself. I thank Him for His grace and His mercy. I thank Him for calling me out of darkness into His marvelous light. How great is our God! Marvelous is He! He's perfect in all His ways! Who wouldn't serve a God like that?!

Call me a sponge. I soaked up the Words of Christ. I did as my leaders instructed. Obedience was second nature. I stayed busy in the church. I joined the gospel choir at my new school. I even sang alto in the church choir. My leaders then used to tell us, 'An idle mind is the devil's workshop.' They told us to get busy and stay busy. We would hang out with other teenagers from nearby churches. From 7 to 11 every Friday night we would go to Saints Roller Rink where we roller-skated to gospel music. Sunday evening we would go to hear the nightly broadcast at Lively Stone Church of God off Saint Louis Avenue. After service was over we would fellowship with each other in the parking lot until the security guard gave the signal for us to roll out. It encouraged me to see other teenagers praising God and living saved. Those were good times.

The time came when God required me to change my friends. This was my struggle. I only had one or two who I thought were real friends. But every time I would pray, I could hear God saying in my spirit to let them go. I wrestled with this. I didn't understand how a God rich in mercy and love wanted me to let go of something I held so dear. How could He require me to let go of the one or two friends I had when they were all I had to begin with? I will be honest with you; my heart was broken. I cried many tears. I tried negotiating with God. I thought maybe I could reach them. I thought maybe I could save them, just as God had saved me.

If I said that the next day we weren't friends anymore that would not be truthful. If I said that we parted ways immediately that would be a lie. But God allowed me to see for myself what the friendship really was. All the mental abuse, the put-downs, the manipulation and control tactics didn't seem so 'appealing' anymore. Now that I was saved, our interests were different too. I wanted to go to church, my friend wanted to hang out with older boys. I wanted to talk about God, she wanted to talk about shameful things. She wanted to swear, I didn't do those things anymore. This was no longer the direction I wanted to go in life. It was as if I wanted to go left she wanted to go right. It seemed we were complete opposites now.

'Therefore if any man be in Christ, he is a new creature: old things are passed away; behold, all things are become new.' (2 Corinthians 5:17)

But even being a baby saint as some called it; I knew my worship, my praise, and even my singing in the choir meant nothing without obedience. How could I lift my hands in worship and not yield my heart wholly to God? How dare I say I am a follower of Christ and not follow His Word? How could I say I love God and not obey his voice?

'...Behold, to obey is better than sacrifice, and to hearken than the fat of rams.' (1 Samuel 15:22)

I am amazed how God can orchestrate even the smallest

details of our life down to the very second. I tried on several attempts to hold on, then let go; hold on again and then let go; a vicious cycle. It did me no good to think I could outwit God. The plans of God are astonishing! Eventually, we changed schools. God created the distance and now that I am older I can see that. The more I dug deeper into living for God and the things of God, the further away these few friends and I became. Until one day the friendship was non-existent. I'm not saying I was perfect. I could never say that. Yet I knew the hand of God was upon me.

There's no sob story here. Where I lost those few friends that I thought I needed, God gave double with the girls from the church. We called ourselves, 'Four Sanctified Girls on a Mission' a friendship that would later prove to hold true.

'But my God shall supply all your needs according to his riches in glory by Christ Jesus.' (Philippians 4:19)

Down through the years I always felt like the outsider to everyone around me. Even now there are some that mock the uniqueness of my character. I didn't dress like everyone. I knew a little bit about fashion but I rarely followed trends. I talked differently and carried myself in a different manner than others. As much as I had my own individuality; I resented being the odd ball. I wanted to fit in. I know what you are thinking. Yes, I was saved, full of the Holy Ghost, speaking in tongues, and on fire for God; but I was still a child. I was still a teenager.

I didn't understand then that it was a blessing to be different, to stand out. As people of God we are meant to be peculiar. We are the light that shines bright in a dark world. We are created to be the city on a hill. We are meant to be set apart from the world. We don't blend in and that's okay. Stand out! Be who God called you to be!

'But ye are a chosen generation, a royal priesthood, an holy nation, a peculiar people; that ye should shew forth the praises of him who hath called you out of darkness into his marvelous light.' (1 Peter 2:9)

I encourage you child of God, don't allow what others think of you to hinder you. People cannot determine who you are. They don't hold that authority over you; God does. It took me several years to come to terms with this. Your diversity is a blessing.

My heart was fixed. My mind made up. I was in too deep. You know how you meet 'the one?' The one you decide to give your heart to. The one you fall in love with. For a man, it's when he finds the woman he will propose to. For that woman, she can see herself with the man who will become her future. I found that in God. I didn't want anything else. Sixteen years old and suddenly life all made sense.

I remember one Sunday during testimony service, I testified about how much I loved God. I was all choked up. I couldn't find the right words. All eyes were on me. So I said, just as in the popular movie Mary Poppins, 'I love God supercalifragilisticexpialidocious.' I couldn't find the words. I felt like Moses. I could not articulate just how much I loved God. I was not ashamed to be saved. I was not ashamed of my salvation. Jesus changed my whole world.

'For I am not ashamed of the gospel of Christ: for it is the power of God unto salvation to every one that believeth; to the Jew first, and also to the Greek.' (Romans. 1:16)

To stay focused, the girls from the church, my sister, and I would often buddy up. It's imperative as children of God that we link up with those who are like-minded, that we surround ourselves with the saints. In order to stay strong in Christ, you've got to be around strong people; those who will help you grow in God. The Bible tells us,

'Iron sharpeneth iron; so a man sharpeneth the countenance of his friend.' (Proverbs 27:17).

We spent most of our free time studying together, having sleepovers, and encouraging each other. We held each other accountable. We even had a prayer line where we would pray for and with each other.

Once during this prayer hour, one of the girls from the church and I were praying on the phone. I remember lying on my bedroom floor with my face down, crying out to God. God had blessed my mother to be saved as well and later allowed her to purchase her own home.

It was while I was praying, that like one closes and open their eyes after a blindfold is taken off, my eyes seemed to open. Not my natural eyes. There seemed to be a foggy and misty atmosphere around me. I didn't know where I was but I kept hearing a distant soft cry. I walked around until I noticed there was a deep hole in the ground. A deep hole like a well had been there.

The closer I came to the hole, the louder the soft cries became. As I glanced into the hole in the ground, I saw a small hurt lamb. It seemed as if it had a few spots of blood on it. I looked around frantically for someone to help me; for someone who could hear the hurting lamb too. However, I was the only one able to see it. There was no one else around. I kept trying to reach down to pull it up but it was too far down.

Eventually, I got down on my knees and tried calling to the lamb. As I knelt down, the lamb turned into a man. A man balled into a fetal position just as the lamb. This startled me. To see such a sight shook me. Immediately I jumped back and my natural eyes were opened. When I opened my eyes, I realized that as I was reaching for the lamb, I was reaching under my bed. I didn't understand.

I couldn't wait to tell my pastor. I didn't know what to make of what happened to me. He told me to write it down and to take it to God in prayer. I opened my notebook and I did just that. I didn't know then, but this was my first vision.

'And it shall come to pass afterwards, that I will pour out my spirit upon all flesh; and your sons and daughters shall prophesy, your old men shall dream dreams, your men shall see visions.' (Joel 2:28)

It took some time for me to understand it all but I kept praying. I kept reading. I kept studying. Before I realized it, days turned into months and as I began to mature in Christ God revealed my first vision. God allowed me to understand that I was an instrument to aid the wounded and to care for those hurting. I was the prophet to hear and see about His people. The door was opened; all I had to do now was to walk through it.

'The Spirit of the Lord God is upon me; because the Lord hath appointed me to preach good tidings unto the meek; he hath sent me to bind up the brokenhearted, to proclaim liberty to the captives, and the opening of the prison to them that are bound; to proclaim the accepta-ble year of the Lord, and the day of vengeance of our God; to comfort all that mourn.' (Isaiah 61:1-2)

Chapter 2: *Understanding the Call*

Whoever said that being a preacher was easy didn't walk a day in my shoes. Being called to preach is more than hulking and hollering; and prophesying is more than foretelling things to come. See, anybody can preach and prophesy. It's the anointing that makes the difference. I was only 18 years old when God called me to the ministry. God spoke to me while I was studying from the book of Isaiah 43:

> '*¹But now thus saith the Lord that created thee, O Jacob, and he that formed thee, O Israel, Fear not: for I have redeemed thee, I have called thee by name; thou art mine. ² When thou passest through the waters, I will be with thee; and through the rivers, they shall not overflow thee: When thou walkest through the fire, thou shalt not be burned; neither shall the flame kindle upon thee.*'

God assured me, no matter what I am with you; that I am for you and I call you by name, go forth. This was my confirmation.

Even though I was young, it was mind blowing that God saw in me what I could not always see in myself.

'... for the Lord seeth not as man seeth; for man looketh on the outward appearance, but the Lord looketh on the heart,' (I Samuel 16:7)

Again, I encourage you, child of God. Know that God can use you at any stage of your life; young or old. God isn't concerned with how long you have been saved; who you know; or where you came from. That's all irrelevant. Those are things man looks at. Don't allow the enemy to come in and set up camp in your mind, to cause you to not know who you are. It's a trick of the enemy to cause you to down play your role in the kingdom. I prophesy now, there's Greatness in you!

Once I surrendered my life to Christ, the calling of a minister appealed to me. I looked at other ministers and I wanted that same anointing. How many of you know: we should be careful what we pray for…because you just might get it?

Coming up in the church, there was a cliché that lingered in the sanctuary. 'The greater the level, the greater the devil.' I thought this didn't really apply to me because I wanted the call. I wasn't like others. See, I wanted to level up. I wanted to minister. I wanted to serve. I loved the people of God. Even more, I loved God…and this love would carry me through.

How many of you can testify God's love isn't like any other love? With both hands raised, I can! This was unlike human love. It was supernatural...indescribable. The very thing I had longed for, I finally found. The mere thought just to know that God loved me even before I loved Him. Whew! So, amazing!

'We love Him, because He first loved us.' (I John 4:19)

Therefore, I was willing to risk it all. God chose me. What an honor! This love made me jump with my eyes wide open. My mind was made up. New level, here I come!

I went through many transitions in my life. Storms were brewing on every hand. I lost some things. I lost some people too. I faced much ridicule and opposition from those close to me. Some even walked away. What I do know now is, there will be times in your life that God will strip you and separate you from anything and anyone who is not connected to your destiny. Understand this, it's not meant for everyone to be part of your forever. Some people only serve a season and a purpose in your life. And, just like winter changes to spring, so do those people. While we try to hang on to possessions and people, thinking that we can't live without them; God has already purposed to replace what was lost with what's better.

It was also during those times that I got married. I became a mother. I truly felt despite it all, I was a blessed woman of God. I had found my niche; I was doing all that God required of me. I taught Sunday school. I helped in outreach. I paid my tithes and offerings. I was faithful to church. I lived a saved life. I waited on God and saved myself for my husband. I was a virgin when I got married. I read my Bible. I prayed and fasted. I worked the tarry room. I visited the sick.

'And now, Israel, what doth the Lord thy God require of thee, but to fear the Lord thy God, to walk in all his ways, and to love him, and to serve the Lord thy God with all thy heart and with all thy soul…,' (Deuteronomy 10:12)

These were my thoughts.

It was after my second daughter that God called me to evangelize. After going through so many storms; some that almost shook my faith so that I wasn't sure if I was up for it. My husband lost his job while I was pregnant with our first child. Days before we had just purchased a family car and I went on maternity leave from my job. We had to move from our high end apartment and live with different family members in the basement of their homes. All our possessions were stored here and there. Then, after much consideration, my husband and I left the ministry where I was born spiritually almost 10 years earlier and to just let it all go was a nightmare for me. To top it off, things didn't end well for us there. There were some family and friends that stopped speaking to us. The storms kept brewing. In 2008 we purchased our first home. We were amazed how fast God was turning things around for us. In 2011 we decided to go for a loan modification with these highly recommended out-of-town lawyers. We didn't know they were swindlers. We didn't know they were just taking our money and not acting on our behalf with the mortgage company. We were young and we trusted them. Not even three years from us getting the keys, we found ourselves in foreclosure. This caused me much heartache. I was embarrassed. I couldn't understand all the whys. Why God allowed it? Why did it have to happen to us? Why did life go this way? Why me God?

Hear me out; people will look at your current situation. They will look at the tests and trials you are going through and say to themselves, 'They must've done something wrong. God must be angry. They must have lost the favor of God.' But I beg to differ. Jesus' disciples asked him in John 9:2-3:

'Who sinned This man or his parents that he was born blind? Jesus answered, neither hath this man sinned, nor his parents: but that the works of God should be made manifest in him.'

When you have served God with all your heart and walked upright before Him, when you know you have been faithful and obedient and totally sold out for Jesus…then you must tell yourself that God is up to something. Things are not as they seem. I didn't know this then.

All the while, the Holy Ghost kept nudging me. The dreams kept occurring. I was like Jonah with nowhere to run. Who did I think I was fooling? So, I waved my white flag. God, I surrender. I came to the understanding that you could never do enough for God. There's no benchmark in Holiness where you can just 'play it safe.' Every day we strive for the mastery. The Apostle Paul said:

'Brethren, I count not myself to have apprehended: but this one thing I do, forgetting those things which are behind, and reaching forth unto those things which are before...,' (Philippians 3:13)

God was telling me to move and it was my time to move. We go from level to level, glory to glory, higher and higher.

Like a flooded river, over the years the dreams kept coming. Each vision was now clearer than the last. God was speaking loudly. He was knocking at my door.

'Behold I stand at the door, and knock: if any man hear my voice, and open the door, I will come in to him and will sup with him, and he with me.' (Revelation 3:20)

God was calling me again, this time to prophecy.

My sisters and brothers, can I lay my cards on the table? I expose my heart to you as I write this. Prophesy is a whole other realm. It's a calling you had better make sure is from God. The Apostle Peter tells us,

'Wherefore the rather, brethren, give diligence to make your calling and election sure: for if ye do these things, ye shall never fail.' (2 Peter 1: 10)

People of God beware! There are those who can speak eloquently and use big fancy words, have a degree or a title and folks will flock to hear that preacher. Even more so, you have some who try to manipulate the gift or the people of God who will say they come in the name of Christ. They will stir you up, build your emotions, declare you are healed and delivered, and yet have no power (Holy Ghost) behind them. The Apostle Paul warns in 2 Timothy 3:5,

'Having a form of godliness, but denying the power thereof: from such turn away.'

In spite of that, to prophesy ... my God, my God! There is no gray area. It's black or white. It's left or right. And you best believe, if nothing else, it's certainly true or false.

When you prophesy, when you say, 'I am a prophet or a prophetess' you are declaring to the people of God, to the un-believers that you are God's mouthpiece. You are proclaiming that the very words you speak are the truth and divinely given by God himself.

'24But if all prophesy, and there come in one that be-lieveth not, or one unlearned, he is convinced of all, he is judged of all: 25And thus the secrets of his heart made manifest, and so falling down on his face he will wor-ship God, and report that God is in you of a truth,' (1 Corinthians 14: 24-25)

So, before stepping into those shoes, I fasted. I laid before God and petitioned Him to hear my cry. I studied. I wanted to know more. This calling was not to be taken lightly, that's for sure.

You may say I was foolish and yeah, at the time, this was where my mind was. I wanted to be sure God knew whom He was calling. He was calling Natisha Wilson: the girl who grew up in the city; the girl with the parents who would later divorce; the one who lost so much and wasn't that popular; the girl who had to quit college less than one year from her degree. That's another story. I couldn't understand why God wanted me. How could He entrust me to do something that was so precious, so profound, and so intimate? I felt so unworthy.

Can I be real for a moment? Growing up I struggled with low self-esteem. Family and friends would always find a way to comment about my size. It didn't matter what I had accomplished. My size was always a backstage factor. I remember overhearing a preacher saying that I was pretty but pretty in the face. Then you add my parents separating when I was still young. My father started drinking shortly after the military and ended being an alcoholic. This was something passed down generation to generation. Even though I have never had an alcoholic drink in my life, family members would say to my sister and me, that we were going to be just like my father and his sister…who struggled off and on with drugs. Some things you never forget. Those words cut like a knife. If you aren't careful the enemy will have you believing the lies he tells, crippling your faith in God before your feet even hit the ground.

The Bible tells us to watch as well as pray because our adversary, the devil goes about as a roaring lion seeking whom he may devour. (Read 1 Peter 5:8)   See, people think that they can speak in any way and say anything about your life and they believe what they are saying is for your good, to help you. They will speak lies, curses, sicknesses and God knows what else over you. And if you are not watching, not being fully aware, you will believe these things. Declare and decree today, that their perception is not who I am. I am who God says I am!

Let me serve notice, if you are one of the ones who are guilty. Repent! Say, I am sorry; even better, apologize. Don't make excuses. There are those who have believed the lies, the words, and the comments spoken over their life and died. Some are suicidal. Some have walked around being tormented in their mind. This is nothing but a trick of the enemy! I thank God who allowed me to overcome the hurt! I thank God who pulled me through! I thank God that the words they uttered…that were designed to kill me did nothing but bless me! For what the enemy meant for my bad, God meant for my good.

> '*And we know that all things work together for good to them that love God, to them who are the called according to his purpose*,' (Romans 8:28)

As much as I like to say I was unaware, without warning my Holy Ghost was stirring like a whirlwind the night before when I was praying and reading my Bible. Even in my sleep God was revealing things to me. I felt like David:

> '*⁷Whither shall I go from thy spirit? Or whither shall I flee from thy presence? ⁸If I ascend up into heaven,*

thou are there: if I make my bed in hell, behold, thou
are there.' (Psalms 139 7:8)

Though I was sound asleep, my spirit was wide awake
communing with God.

On one occasion, it was like any given Sunday morning at
Lighthouse; the saints were in high praise, and yes, the children
too. There's no discrimination here.

'Let everything that hath breath praise the Lord. Praise
ye the Lord.' (Psalms 150:6)

The music was going and the saints were dancing before
God. What I thought was going to be just another service; I
suddenly felt an unexplainable presence come over me. The
anointing was so thick in the sanctuary.

My God! My God! When I tried to stand, I tried shaking
the feeling off but the weight of the Glory of God knocked me
off my feet. I lay there slain in the Spirit, on my face before
God. What were truly only a few moments in time really felt
like an eternity. The Spirit of the Lord began to pour heavily
into my spirit. Finally, when I was able to stand, my feet felt
heavy. It felt like electricity flowed through my body from the
inside out. The Spirit of the Lord spoke to me and said, 'Prophesy.' My spirit felt so full at that moment. The moment I
opened my mouth I began to speak what thus said the Lord. I
prophesied under the unction of the Holy Ghost, both blessings
and warnings, rebukes and promises. My Spirit then felt at rest.

Yes, it was I prophesying. Here I was. I felt as if I was

watching myself in slow motion, like an out of body experience. It seemed so surreal. I was in awe of the power of God. I've seen great preachers preach the house down. I've seen evangelist unction in the Holy Ghost and evangelize from city to city. I had even seen other prophets and prophetesses before me prophecy, declaring God's words with divine authority. However, it's completely different when it's you. See, you know you, but obviously not like God knows you.

'For I know the thoughts that I think toward you, saith the Lord, thoughts of peace, and not of evil, to give you an expected end.' (Jeremiah 29:11)

You know how you think you know everything about God; not literally everything but you get what I am saying. You know the details of the Creation, you know your favorite Psalms by heart, you know the birth of Jesus, you even know the life of Paul; but you never really know God in His fullness. We're ever learning. There's so much to know of God and the ways of God. I've been saved a long time but the feeling of the Spirit of God in that capacity was jaw-dropping, unmeasurable, without words to do it justice.

The Bible tells us in Proverbs 4:7,

'Wisdom is the principal thing; therefore get wisdom: and with all thy getting get an understanding.'

I am not one who pretends to always know or understand the ways and moves of God. No, that's not me. There are times when it's simply beyond our finite minds and reasoning, and that's okay. Yet one thing is for certain, it was rooted deep in my heart to understand the call, the gift to prophesy. So, like any other time I found myself praying and fasting. I needed to consecrate myself before Him, to come before Him humble, as I knew how. The Holy Ghost instructed me to study the prophet Jeremiah.

I found myself reading the same passages and chapters over and over. It seemed to be so overwhelming at first. What I didn't expect was the more I read it, it began to become clearer as if I was reading the journal of an old friend. This caught me completely off guard.

Now wait a minute, let's be truthful. We have all had times where no matter how many times we tried to do something or attempt to, it seemed we were farther than we first began. And if we could be transparent for a moment, we would be truthful to say we found ourselves frustrated with the process from time to time.

What's so amazing about God, He comes in just at the right time! Before I realized it my understanding opened up. I was an open book. The prophet's words and God's instruction were like finding the last piece to the puzzle. Aha! My heart swelled and my mind started flowing. God was speaking and finally, I began to understand this thing called prophecy. It was a lot to take in and even now it still can be. I found myself thirsty for God. My spirit yearned to know Him, to learn of Him. The question now, was I willing?

Chapter 3: *Fear of Prophecy*

You can only run for so long until one day you have to face your fears whether you're ready or not. I was tired of running but I was definitely not ready. See, for some they fear spiders, heights, being alone, and any number of things; but for me, here I was, amazed but afraid of the gift to prophesy.

Move! Keep going. Keep pressing. Don't give up! Push. Push harder. Take just a few more steps. You can make it. This is what my inner man, my Holy Ghost was telling me. In my heart I knew what was right. In my heart I knew where God was leading me. I knew God was saying move. And though my heart fluttered at the presence of God, my feet were stiff like a tire stuck in the mud.

Let me guess, you may ask how you can be so foolish? You may shake your head and say, move it, get out the way. I can do better. But I caution you to realize that the grass is not always greener on the other side. I pray you understand that what God has for you is only for you. Don't chase titles and don't covet anyone else's anointing. For every anointing please know there is a cost for the power and a testimony behind it.

'... *From everyone to whom much has been given, much will be required...*' (Luke 12:48)

As much as it sounds contrary, I did want God. My heart was at a crossroads. I petitioned God. I prayed, 'Lord you know that I love you. It's just that I went through so much pain, so much heartache this far. I've lost a lot down through the years." See, I was tired of all the hurting and crying. I didn't want to be the basis of other folk's jokes. I was tired of my name being passed around the church like a bad apple. Here I was in my thirties and I felt like I did when I was younger. I wanted to blend in.

Truth be told, we have all been there...one time or another. Have you ever petitioned God trying to bargain with Him? So you haven't played the role of negotiator; hoping to negotiate the terms of your life? Have you ever wanted to dictate when God moves and how He moved? You ever tell God, I need you to move NOW, not tomorrow? If we could just be real for once?! Examine your own heart. Sometimes you can find what God is asking you to do downright difficult. You can fool people some of the time, but I guarantee you can't fool God anytime.

The reason why some of us remain bound is because we are ashamed of what others will think when they learn of our struggle. We're too dignified. You can fake like you never begged God. You can lie and say you always followed through.

But God knoweth all things. Jesus said in John 8:36,

> *'If the Son therefore shall make you free, ye shall be free indeed.'*

Hence, that's the very reason we come to church Sunday after Sunday. We sing in the choir, we lift our hands, we encourage others and STILL we're bound and chained.

Trust me, you are not alone. I too have done things God has told me to, things that have caused me ridicule, heartbreak, and much pain; but have done so out of obedience. I can be honest with where I am and who I am in God. Still, here I was once again; the Spirit of the Lord wouldn't easily let go.

Stay with me. I know of some truly great, anointed and powerful men and women of God. I could easily see how the power of God rested on them. They were sold out to Christ, gung-ho for Jesus. Nevertheless, I've also seen some of the trials they went through. I've seen their heartaches. I knew pieces of their story. I was already going through many of my own storms. I thought foolishly to myself that this life wasn't for me. Try to understand, you may see the woman I am now but you fail to understand the girl that came first.

> *'Yea, and all that will live godly in Christ Jesus shall suffer persecution.'* (2 Timothy 3:12)

We are intricately designed and created in the image of God. Though we are all unique in our own way, one thing is for certain and two for sure, fear is not a part of our genetic make-up or DNA. You have to understand, fear is a spirit. The enemy uses it as a tactic, a tool to destroy us. Fear has a way of sucking the life out of you until there is nothing left but a hollow shell. It is known to kill dreams before they are even set in motion. Imagine you are the one who desires to start your own business. God has given you the green light. You have the blue prints all mapped out in your mind. You've done the research and you're ready to take that leap of faith. Oh, but here comes fear and without warning you began to doubt. The fear of failure creeps in your heart and you lose sight of the vision. It can cause a person anxiety, depression, anger, loneliness and even worse, suicide. Let me make it clear, fear is a poison that once it's ingested it seizes every part of your body, rendering you incapable of moving forward. Now you're spiritually paralyzed. This is fear at its finest.

'For God hath not given us the spirit of fear; but of power, and of love, and of a sound mind.' (2 Timothy 1:7)

I remember, even as a child, fear had repeatedly taunted me. As a little girl and well into my late teens, early twenties I was afraid of the dark. So much so, that I could not sleep without a nightlight. Fear caused me to endure the physical, sexual, and verbal abuse from other kids on the school bus and never say a word to anyone. Fear said to me as a young woman because you are overweight, you will never find love. When I got married, fear whispered because you always wanted to be a mother, you will never conceive. Just when I thought fear had done all its damage, the same fear asked me, 'Who are you to prophesy? You're not worthy. There are better candidates. You're not special. You're not really a prophet.'

Just in case you weren't aware or no one ever told you, you can't operate in fear and yet have faith. The two cannot and will not coexist simultaneously. Real faith drives out fear. Imagine mixing water and oil together in a glass. No matter how you stir it or shake it up, the two will never become one. It's a simple understanding, science 101. So it is with faith and fear. My faith was slipping from me. I wanted to trust God. I really wanted to be obedient. However, fear was the oil in my life. I felt like Asaph, in the 73rd chapter of Psalms,

'[1]But as for me, my feet were almost gone, my steps had well nigh slipped.'

I hold nothing back when I tell you at that moment; I believed Satan's lies. Fear had its claws in me deep and was going for the kill. I looked at my past and I looked at my current situation and thought, God had chosen the wrong one. Who was I? All the words people had spoken against me to hurt me surfaced like a small log in a rushing river. And just that quick, I forgot the promises of God and all He told me.

'For all the promise of God in him are yea, and in him Amen, unto the glory of God by us.' (2 Corinthians 1:20)

It's true. Yes, I was saved. Yes, I was sanctified and filled with the Holy Ghost. I was anointed but here I was, just like Jonah, just like Jeremiah, running like Elijah…running from the call. I thought I knew what was best for my life. The Bible tells us,

> '*Trust in the Lord with all thine heart; and lean not unto thine own understanding.*' (Proverbs 3:5)

You don't have to say it, I will. I was beside myself…to think I knew what was best for my life. The audacity! The nerve!

As a body we must be careful not to allow pride to consume us. It can cause us to think more highly than we ought. (See Romans 12:3). In the same breath we rebuke or judge another, it's in the next breath we ourselves are judged by the Word of God. For instance, where I may struggle to obey, you may struggle with lying. Where I have overcome depression, another may overcome fornication. My sister in the Lord may struggle with being faithful while the next sister has no issues being present when the church doors open but still she may struggle with her flesh. That's why it behooves us to pray for one another. You never know what battle your brother or sister may fight in their flesh.

> '*Brethren, if a man be overtaken in a fault, ye which are spiritual, restore such an one in the spirit of meekness; considering thyself, lest thou also be tempted.*' (Galatians 6:1)

I tried to visualize that God was not speaking to me, that He wasn't calling me higher. However, the more I pretended, the more I thought I was hiding from God; the more the Spirit of God endowed me with His unfailing love. He consumed my thoughts. His grace followed me. His mercy overwhelmed me. I was mesmerized by His amazing love. Now wait, there are those who will read this chapter and say had I been God, I would've chosen someone else; what a waste of time. But that's the reason man is not God and God is God all by Himself. He doesn't need your commentary. Period! Man can look at where you're at and deem you unworthy, useless, unfit. Yet, what wins me every single time is not the cars, it's not the houses. Forget the notoriety. It's not even the money. It's His undying love! See it's not what he does for me, but because of who he is to me. He's just God like that!!

Even with the conflict brewing inside of me; and when I say brewing, yes, it was stirring…stirring like a hurricane. Again, God kept speaking to me. I was torn. I felt as Paul,

'I find then a law, that, when I would do good, evil is present with me.' (Romans 7:21)

I was at the point of no return. I had been saved too long, not to know better, to think I was in charge of my life. One night God spoke to me in my spirit. He said, 'You have a choice. Choose fear or choose love.' God let me know that I couldn't keep using fear as a reason for not being obedient.

'... How long halt ye between two opinions? If the Lord

be God, follow him: but if Baal, then follow him...' (I Kings 18:21)

So I called myself appealing to God's better nature. Yes, that's right. So I prayed,

'God, it's just me. Here I am humble before you. Lord, this season in my life seems to be so frustrating. Father, I love you with my whole heart but I am scared. I am not articulate. Sometimes my words get mixed up. God you know I don't have degree after degree. I want to be obedient in all things. But this fear feels real.'

I thought I knew in what way God was going to answer my prayer. I thought God would butter me up and tell me everything will be all right, that I was off the hook. But He didn't. The Spirit of the Lord chastened me. The rebuke was real.

'⁶Then said I, Ah, Lord God! Behold I cannot speak: for I am a child. ⁷But the Lord said unto me, Say not, I am a child: for thou shalt go to all that I shall send thee, and whatsoever I command thee thou shalt speak. ⁸Be not afraid of their faces: for I am with thee to deliver thee, saith the Lord.' (Jeremiah 1:6-8)

When I tell you it was as if God shook me himself. Believe me. My Holy Ghost stood up in me and just like a lieutenant gives a solider his orders, God had my full attention. The Spirit of the Lord was telling me to get it together. No more excuses. Stand firm. Prepare yourself!

'Moreover whom he did predestinate, them he also called: and whom he called, them he also justified: and whom he justified, them he also glorified.' (Romans 8:30)

Just like the prodigal son, I came to myself. (Read Luke 15). I came to my senses. I had an epiphany! With God, I always win. I always come out on top. When it looks like I am failing, I am actually winning. There is no failure in God. I am destined by God for greatness. I am a weapon for the kingdom…therefore I must fight like never before and not buckle.

'The Lord is my light and my salvation; whom shall I fear? The Lord is the strength of my life; of whom shall I be afraid?' (Psalms 27:1)

Man and woman of God, let me speak life to you. If you have ever walked in my shoes, if you have ever been afraid of the call on your life, then let me encourage you today. Shake yourself! Speak the words of life and not death. Look back over your life, flip back year by year and see that God has never let you down before. Though the vision tarries, wait on the Lord. I declare and decree by faith this day, no more fear. No more anxiety. The nightmares are over. Your deliverance is here! Understand this; His glory is manifested in your tears, manifested in your pain, manifested in your suffering. So, trust the process & not the pain. I prophesy now. Those that hurt you, used you, talked about you will have no other choice but to see the glory of God revealed in your life.

Solider, yes you…for you are a solider in the army of the Lord. I don't care what the enemy has said. I don't care what folks may have done. Let the past be the past. Open your mouth and speak these very words. Repeat these words after me. I will not be carried away by my own emotions. My thoughts are not like God, for He knows what's best for me. I will not let my enemy see me sweat. God will help me and that right early. He will deliver me with a strong hand! He will strengthen me for the call. He has given me the authority to perform all that He has called me to do. I am no longer bound. God is with me! He is not against me. He will help me…for I am a prophet to the nations. Worry is gone! Fear is gone! For I am fearless and I declare I am free.

'*And from the days of John the Baptist until now the kingdom of heaven suffereth violence, and the violent take it by force.*' (Matthew 11:12)

Chapter 4: Accepting the Gift

Lights! Camera! Action! These are the three words that are echoed on every movie set with big bright lights, cameras rolling in motion and everyone in their rightful position. Still, after putting forth all the hard work, an actor's lifetime achievement is the hopeful expectation of being awarded an honorary gift or a medal of honor. Then, after being awarded with such, it's still up to the actor or actress to accept this exceptional gift. I found myself in similar shoes. All of my life I wanted to be a part of something. I longed to be accepted. However, here it was God had granted me the privilege of being His mouthpiece. He gave me the gift to prophesy, an anointing and gift I could never repay. Hence tragically, I found myself hesitant to receive such a gift. When God called me to the next level in ministry, giving me this prophetic gift, in the Spirit I signed my name on the dotted line. "Yes, I Natisha Wilson do hereby solemnly accept the terms and conditions as a prophet to the nations presented to me this day by our Lord and Savior, Jesus Christ." I finally accepted the call upon my life…or so I thought.

Please hear me out. You know those funky and awkward feelings of being in a state of limbo? You know when you're in between two things? You're certainly not at the end, you're really not at the beginning but you are in some weird place in the middle. Well, yeah, me too. The crazy thing is, if my memory serves me correct; I remember the day I told God yes. I said yes to the call. I said yes to the gift and therefore I expected to move forward in my calling. However, things didn't quite go that way.

Let me try to paint you a picture. See, I was at the starting line and aimed to go. I had my sneakers laced and my sweatband on but when the gun (Spirit) fired and the smoke cleared…there I was. Do you get my drift? I was in limbo. In the Spirit realm, I was no longer at the starting line but I definitely can admit I wasn't sprinting. I was moving in slow motion.

Here I was again. Oh Lord! Tell me not again, this dreadful place. Certainly I thought I was ready. I thought what my words echoed my heart would definitely follow. I was completely wrong. Geesh! I signed up for the next level in God. I entered this Christian race but I didn't read all the fine print. Somehow and somewhere I forgot the promises of God. Somehow and somewhere I misplaced my trust in God. Where was my faith? Where was my "yes"?

Please try to understand that this Christian journey is no ordinary race. It's more than just that. It's a spiritual race to the finish (Heaven). It's not a race as man seeth nor is it a race to compete or undo the other, for we ought not to compete in the body of Christ. The Bible tells us that we are but one body. No, this is a race to keep moving forward…a race to progress to the kingdom of God at any cost and by any means necessary. Oh, I was definitely in the race, this much was true. My life duty was to keep running no matter what. I was to keep running amid the disappointments, the discouragement, the heartaches and pains. However, I was stalling the progression.

'Know ye not that they which run in a race run all, but one receiveth the prize? So run, that ye may obtain.' (1 Corinthians 9:24)

Sometimes in life you can have the best intentions and things still go awry. It was never my intention to be in a state of limbo. It was never my intention to stall at the call or ignore the gift of God. I had every intention of obeying. I had every intention of allowing God to have free reign in my life. It was my true intention to stop hiding behind fear and my past. I had every intention to operate in my gift. Trust me when I say, I had every intention to prophecy and heed the voice of the Lord. But sometimes our well thought out intentions don't always go as planned; this I can attest to.

See, when the day comes for the homeowner to sign the bank contract on the purchase of their new home, they never foresee that later down the road they may lose their job. Embarrassed and heartbroken they later face the possibility of foreclosure. Perhaps you'll better understand this, imagine the newly married couple on their wedding day, both are in love as they take their vows before family and God. They never intend years later that their spouse would have an affair and what was once a 'perfect' marriage quickly dissolves in divorce. The love that was once so precious now seems tarnished and gone forever.

My sisters, my brothers what I am saying is this, find me one person in the body of Christ or in this world for that matter who can honestly and boldly declare every intention they had whether good or bad always went as planned. I guarantee you won't find one. Your average person does not wake up in the morning and plan to do the very opposite of what they expect to do. Yet we all know, life happens and we aren't perfect. Paul wrote,

'As it is written, There is none righteous, no, not one.' (Romans 3:10)

After acknowledging the prophetic call on my life, for a season I yielded myself wholly to the Spirit of God. Whenever God said speak, I spoke. I would prophesy under the unction of the Holy Ghost. I allowed God to use me at His will. Yet just like summer turns to fall, there was a change in my spirit. I suddenly became like the apostle Peter when Jesus called him to come and join Him out on the water. (Read Matthew 14). Foolishly, I looked at others. I took my eyes off Christ. I saw their anointing. I saw their gifts and talents. Suddenly, I began to sink.

'But when he saw the wind boisterous, he was afraid; and beginning to sink, he cried, saying, Lord, save me.'

(Matthew 14:30)

Some of us go through this life wearing ourselves down by trying to please or be accepted by others. It may be those far or near to us, even our dear friends and family. Let me be the one to try to spare you from heartache and disappointment. In this life, no matter how hard you try; you cannot please everyone all the time. There will always be those who may not accept the call on your life. I urge you don't stress about it! It's okay. The one and only person that truly matters is Jesus Christ our Lord. If God called you, that's all that matters whether folks accept your calling or not. So my brothers and sisters it's okay to let go and trust God. Salvation is a learning process regardless of title. I admonish you to look to Jesus. He knows all things!

If you have read chapter 3 and now are reading this, you may pose a question in your mind. I thought she accepted the call on her life? Well yeah, I did too. Still what baffles me the most is the fact I'm not quite sure just how I ended up here; this place of uncertainty. Maybe you are the person who's sure of yourself, sure of the call that's upon your life and embraced who God said you are? If that's you then I commend you great-ly. To God be the glory! Truly, I mean that. However, I am appealing to you, that one who struggles in the Spirit to say a simple 'Yes Lord' come what may. You may further ask me and expect a clear answer…well do you? Do you accept the call? Truthfully I am sure of this one thing above all else…that I love God more than life itself. I love God with every part of my being. Even more so, I am sure that I am called and chosen of God. The challenge before me is about acceptance.

As I look back to when I was a little girl, Momma never promised me this life would be easy. The preached never said everyday would be filled with sunshine. In fact the Bible tells us,

'*all that will live godly in Christ Jesus shall suffer persecution.*' (2 Timothy 3:12)

It comes with the territory of being saved. I've come to terms with that. That's why it's imperative that we remind ourselves daily of the Word of God. It is in the Word of God that we'll find everything we need, from Genesis to Revelation. It's here that we can find solace in reading God's word and to allow it to take root in our very hearts. For all the uncertainty, the problems I faced, my unanswered questions there was an answer to them all...even the uncertainty surrounding my acceptance of this gift. So yes, these words are literally the words of life...for in it are life-changing words.

'*I beseech you therefore, brethren, by the mercies of God, that ye present your bodies a living sacrifice, holy, acceptable unto to God, which is your reasonable service.*' (Romans 12:1)

Apparently, I didn't get the memo. What memo you may ask? The one that reads loud and clear, 'Saying one thing and doing another are two totally different things.' Selah.

Here I am again, laying my heart out on the line to you. Transparency can sometimes bring remorse and pain. Boy, do I know this. Ha! It causes one to become vulnerable, exposed even. The body of Christ today lacks true authenticity. When we are transparent, then and only then, can people be delivered. They can then be healed and truly restored. It hurts me deeply (in my flesh but not in my heart) to share that this is how I felt about my calling. Nevertheless, this is my journey; how I went from prophesy restrained to prophesy unleashed. Therefore, I have purposed in my heart to help somebody (even if it's only one) to embrace the call and not run from it just as I did.

'If we confess our sins, he is faithful and just to forgive us our sins, and to cleanse us from all unrighteous-ness.' (1 John 1:9)

I was at the point where I resented myself. Why did I have to second-guess every single little thing? Why couldn't I be like the others who flew out the gate blazing ready to go and driven viciously by the anointing on their life? I became angry with myself. I was losing my focus. I allowed myself to become discouraged and distracted. Why did I not fully accept the gift…the prophetic call that was upon my life? Ugh. I was playing devil's advocate with my own self. Well, what if they don't receive you? What if they say you're not called? How can you preach and prophesy deliverance to others and be going through (test and trials) at the same time? This tug-o-war was becoming tiresome for me.

Rather than chastened me, the Spirit of the Lord wooed me in the Spirit. It wasn't an outpour of His love that got me this time. No. It was instead His patience and His relentless mercy that seized my heart.

'It is of the Lord's mercies that we are not consumed, because his compassion fail not.' (Lamentations 3:22)

Boom! Boom! Boom! My Spirit man began to bombard me with scriptures one after another to encourage and strength-en me. The Holy Ghost sent scripture after scripture to build me up on most holy faith.

'God forbid: yea, let God be true, but every man a li-ar...' (Romans 3:4)

'If any man will come after me, let him deny himself, and take up his cross and follow me.' (Matthew 16:24)

'For me to live is Christ, and to die is gain.' (Philippi-ans 1:21)

'What shall we then say to these things? If God be for us, who can be against us?' (Romans 8:31)

'Finally, my brethren, be strong in the Lord, and in the power of his might.' (Ephesians 6:10)

Wow! Isn't it phenomenal…the ways of God? How he does what He does when He does it? How our ways are not like His ways? It is so amazing. My God! My God! Truth be told, I really expected God to throw me away. I expected Him to wash his hands of me. I even expected God to choose some-one else or take His gift away altogether. The trouble is some-times we think of God as we think of ourselves. In actuality the two don't even compare. Thank God for mercy! For He is the potter and I am the clay; a vessel for the master's use.

> *'For my thoughts are not your thoughts, neither are your ways my ways, saith the Lord. For as the heavens are higher than the earth, so are my ways higher than your ways, and my thoughts than your thoughts.'* (Isaiah 55:8-9)

Praise be unto God! Truly, I am grateful for the grace of God, for allowing me the opportunity to recognize who I was meant and always destined to be. This same grace allowed me to see that my anointing is my anointing. My calling is my call-ing and my gift is my gift. No one else could give it or take it away. God, all by Himself, had stamped my name on it! I fi-nally accepted who I am. I am set apart and chosen to advance the kingdom of God. This is my destiny.

> *'But by the grace of God I am what I am: and his grace which bestowed upon me was not in vain; but I labored more abundantly than they all: yet not I, but the grace of God which was with me.'* (1 Corinthians 15:10)

There I was all this time struggling to go forward in God…to accept the gift of prophecy and accept the call upon my life, simply because I looked at myself, my flesh that is. I looked at Natisha when instead I should have kept my eyes of God. This was foolish of me. I relied on my own capabilities and strength. When the fact remains unchanged. In all our (human) glory their still lays imperfections and frailties. Ah, it is the grace of God that's upon my life to do what He has called me to do.

'8For by grace are ye saved through faith; and that not of yourselves: it is the gift of God: 9Not of works, lest any man should boast.' (Ephesians 2:8-9)

Let's dissect this thing we call grace. Why does it even matter? What is grace you may ask? What role does it play in our lives? It is defined as being, 'freely given, unmerited favor and love of God.' I don't care what you may think or what you may have heard, we cannot earn God's grace. Grace looks beyond your genealogy and socio-economic status and sees purpose. It ignores the judgment of man and sees your destiny. It is freely given therefore you cannot demand or buy yourself extra grace. No, your money isn't good enough to earn the things of God. Moreover, the dictionary uses the term 'unmerited'. What does that mean? Let me tell you. We aren't worthy of it. It means in all your 'goodness' you still don't deserve it. Grace is the gift of God.

'Who hath saved us, and called us with an holy calling, not according to our works, but according to his own purpose and grace, which was given us in Christ Jesus before the world began.' (2 Timothy 1:9)

Since time had passed, I understand now what I didn't always understand. For so long I walked around with my eyes wide open but in my Spirit I was blind. Now I can say, I see what I didn't always see. All things work according to God's perfect timing. The grace of God was upon me and like David in the twenty-third book of Psalms, it has followed me all the days of my life. I recognize now that despite the trials that may come and the winds that may blow (or my own insecurities) God will carry me through them all. I accept the call to greatness. Therefore I humble myself and pray, *Lord not my will but Thy will be done.*

'And he said unto me, my grace is sufficient for thee: for my strength is made perfect in weakness. Most gladly therefore will I rather glory in my infirmities, that the power of Christ may rest upon me.' (2 Corinthians 12:9)

Isn't it obvious by now? I wasn't born perfect. I hadn't, how do you say it, clocked out of heaven. That's a reality I cannot escape or hide. However, I strive earnestly toward perfection in Christ. Hereby, He is our prime example. God knows I have faults and I've made mistakes along the way but God knows I've also tried. I have been like that ol Zion song, '…like a tree planted by the water, I shall not be moved.' When others fainted, Lord knows I've held on with all that's within me. I may have swayed to the left and perhaps leaned a bit to the right…but I've remained in position. So, yes I wholeheartedly accept the gift and the prophetic call on my life. I no longer put my confidence in my own flesh but in my great big God!

'Therefore, my beloved brethren, be ye steadfast, unmovable, always abounding in the work of the Lord, forasmuch as ye know that your labor is not in vain in the Lord.' (1 Corinthians 15:58)

Man of God and Woman of God don't allow your past or your own shortcomings hinder you from being who God has called you to be. Our prayer should always be, *'God help me to see me as you see me.'* My friend, be strong. I say, be courageous. Get up from where you are! Surely if God called you, He will equip you! He knows your ending before you even begin. No matter how long it takes you to get there…just make sure you get there. God doesn't start what He doesn't finish. He will see you through. You don't have to learn the hard way or stall as I did but allow me to help you. Acceptance and perception works hand in hand. You cannot accept every little thing you see. Sometimes our fleshly eyes will fail us. Build your hope on the Word of God. Look at your life through your spiritual eyes. Learn to speak over yourself! The Bible tells us that life and death lies in the power of the tongue. (Read Proverbs 18) Don't let go of His precious promises, for God is faithful. Hold fast to your dreams. Accept what God allows. Accept the call upon your life whether your ministry is to teach, preach, help, spreading the Word of God, or prophecy. It shall come to pass. God said it and that settles it.

'So shall my word be that goeth forth out of my mouth: it shall not return unto me void, but it shall accomplish that which I please, and it shall prosper in the thing whereto I sent it.' (Isaiah 55:11)

Whatever God has purposed for your life know that it shall come to pass. There's no roadblock, no detour, no gossip, or insecurity that can halt God's plans for your life. The only one that can stop you is YOU! It is the will of God that we are willing and obedient, from the heart and not begrudgingly. It's true, in the beginning, yes, I ran from the call…and so we tend to when we don't completely understand. Still in all of that I've come a mighty long way. No more excuses. I accept the call on my life. I now hold fast to the precious gift God has so entrusted to me. I am a prophet. I vow to no longer take that for granted.

Look at the saints who came before us. Look at Moses who had everything he ever wanted in Egypt under the leadership of Pharaoh. However, after learning his true lineage, born a Jew from a slave woman he accepted the call upon his life. He would later lead the children of Israel out of bondage after four hundred years of slavery and across the Red Sea. Obeying the voice of God, he brought forth the law and the Ten Commandments. When it all boils down, it comes down to one word, acceptance. Let's flip over to the New Testament at the apostle Paul who began his life as Saul. He recklessly persecuted the early church. Zealous and highly educated of the law, following Jewish traditions he bound and imprisoned many of the faith. Yet when Jesus called him, knocking him down blind and later even changing his name…he humbly accepted the call. He asked God, 'What would you have me to do?' (Read Acts 9) As we read further he would go through many tests and was occasionally beaten with many stripes. However, Paul later wrote most of the New Testament and started many churches thereafter preaching the gospel to the Gentiles. I don't care how you try to unravel it, it still comes down to acceptance. Let the record note, it's not how you start but how you finish.

By the grace of God, I've come to truly appreciate and understand just how precious it is to be given the gift of prophecy. It is as delicate and intimate as a budding rose on a vine with thorns and thickets. If we aren't careful to nurture our gift the enemy will choke it out of us. Therefore, I count it an honor and a privilege to serve as a prophet to the nations, (Read the book of Jeremiah) to speak with my voice but allow others to hear God's words. The Bible tells us,

'For many are called, but few are chosen.' (Matthew 22:14)

Forever and a day, I thank God that He loved me enough to choose me. I thank God for His grace. He didn't allow the enemy to triumph over me. God has given us the victory! Just as a knight kneels down before a king, so I bow before God and humbly accept my gift and my calling. Yes, it took me some time, but thank God, I made it!

Chapter 5: *Rejoicing with Praise*

Hey! Hold up! Wait one minute! Let's open up with praise. C'mon put your hands together. Let's celebrate God just being God. Let's start things off right…in praise break mode! I'll be the praise leader. C'mon open up your mouth and exalt our God! Tell God, 'Thank you.' Thank you Lord! Now is not the time to be silent. Give glory to God! His name is Jesus. He's Sovereign and reigns supreme. He is King of kings and Lord of lords. He is The Prince of Peace. He is the one and true living God and for that He deserves your best praise. Don't pull back now. Yeah, that's right, give Him all the glory. C'mon and lift those hands and lift Him higher. He inhabits the praises of His people. Don't stop praising! You're right on the edge of your breakthrough!

'O magnify the Lord with me, and let us exalt his name together.' (Psalms 34:3)

Listen, I find it quite easy to rejoice in God because He has been so good to me. As I look back over my life and see from where God has brought me, I can truly say I am blessed. I can't speak for you; I can only speak for myself. He's a miracle working God! See, it's been a long time coming and considering when I got saved until now as I accept this prophetic calling on my life, it has not always been an easy journey. Yet through it all, God has been more than patient, more than kind and much more than gracious. When I rewind in my mind and think how He's brought me this far, my spirit is so full. He's brought me through the good times and the bad, over the mountains and through the valleys. My God, my God! I can't help but to rejoice!

When I hear the word *rejoice* I began to think of lots of colorful confetti, pretty streamers, and loud sounds of celebration. I think of high praise, clapping, and adoration. The online dictionary defines the word rejoice as, "great joy, happiness, delight, to celebrate, jubilation."

Without question I have a reason to celebrate Jesus. Even more so, I definitely have a reason to praise Him. He called me as His own, a prophet to the nations. He made me his mouthpiece. I am an ambassador of Christ. I am chosen. When my soul was lost in a world full of sin, Christ came and saved me. When folks counted me out, and said I wasn't going to be anybody God made me somebody. There were some that didn't think I would even make it this far; yet God birthed purpose in me. So you see, I have to praise Him.

There was a time in my life were I wasn't even sure if I could make it. For a season there was division in my house; my husband worshipped one place and I another. I battled postpartum depression, my finances were upside down and at the end of the day God still required me to minister and prophesy to the people of God. I have faced many tears and heartaches through the years but I have determined in my heart that I will always give God my undeniably best praise. It's out of love and obedience to Christ that I will always do just that. See, I've made a vow to the Lord and I plan on keeping that vow. You see, despite what I have to go through, I've come to the plain and simple truth. God is worthy and able to do anything but fail. Neither my situation nor my circumstance dictates my worship. I was created for worship. I was created as an instrument of praise.

'I will praise thee, O Lord, with my whole heart; I will shew forth all thy marvelous works.' (Psalms 9:1)

Needless to say, this prophetic calling is Heaven sent and God-given. But, there's a cost for the oil (anointing). Saying yes to God has a price. Sometimes saying yes and in my case running or saying no, will challenge your praise. Don't get me wrong. I treasure the call that's upon my life and I guard my anointing as I would my own natural life. If I have to press out a praise then let me get to pressing. I won't dare murmur or complain. I count it an honor to serve God and to be chosen of Him. So, I will praise Him while I yet have the chance.

Please allow me to be candid for a moment. Anybody can praise God when the sun is shining and the birds are singing. It's easy to praise God and to serve Him when everything in life seems to be going right. What do you mean Prophetess? Often times we find salvation easy when there's extra money to spend, the kids are doing well, you have marital bliss, and the business is taking off. Oh, but when the clouds start rolling in and the thunder sounds, how quickly does our sunshine turn to rain? Can you still praise Him then? When everybody in church knows your family's secrets and your heart is broken but you're the praise team leader…can you still sing to the glory of God? Can you still rejoice in God when you've been humiliated and outcast by those you hold dear? Can you work the altar when you're still waiting on God to answer your prayers? My God, my God!

I then charge you man and woman of God as Paul charged Timothy. Allow nothing…and I mean absolutely nothing or no one to hinder your praise, not even your own self. Know that even your own emotions can sometimes trip you up and hinder you. We should keep our eyes on Jesus Christ. He was the ultimate sacrifice for our sins and therefore we ought to bring the sacrifice of praise. Hard times may come but push through it. Sacrifice through your tears. Sacrifice through your brokenness. I ask you this, where is your sacrifice?

> *'By him therefore let us offer the sacrifice of praise to God continually, that is, the fruit of our lips giving thanks to his name.'* (Hebrews 13:15)

I urge you not to construe my words, child of God. It's God's great pleasure to give us the kingdom and to see you prosper and be in good health. Yet we must make up our minds to rejoice, to celebrate, to praise when we find ourselves on the mountaintop or in the valley low. We must be ready to praise

Him at any given time during whatever season we find ourselves in. It's time out for playing church and just praising God when we feel good. I can hear you. I do understand. 'But Prophetess you don't know what they said about me. You don't know what they did. I have sacrificed. I have suffered loss. You don't understand; it's not easy.' Trust me I know just how you feel. I don't say that lightly and without heart.

You must understand the enemy expects us to curse God and to blame Him for all the mishaps in our life. He does this so when we come into the house of God we don't have a mind to praise God because we're so focus on our issues. Friend, if we aren't careful we will lose our focus. We will look to the left of us and say oh that needs to be fixed in my life. We'll look to the right and say why them and not me. Why did God call her to prophesy? Why did God call him to preach? We will pull straws and think that in this life we have come up short. This could not be further from the truth. The enemy has but one agenda, ultimately, that is to kill, steal, and destroy. Know the enemy's devices. If he can kill your praise then he can steal your joy. If he can steal your joy, he can destroy your faith and hope in God. Even the apostle Paul said if we ONLY have hope in this life, '...*we are men most miserable.*' (1 Corinthians 15:19) Friend, I caution you. We cannot afford to get distracted or to get off course. We must push pass everything else...all the mishaps, all the issues, all the disappointments and push out a praise!

In order to be successful in our spiritual walk, there are some key essentials every believer must have. We must have faith. We must pray. We must consecrate ourselves.

We must praise…and when all is said and done, we must rejoice! Celebrate God and all He has done for us. When we praise God, it's a barrier that protects our minds, protects our hearts, and protects us from the snares of the enemy. Listen to me carefully. I am not saying if we praise God then we won't experience pain or heartache in this life. No, that's not what I am suggesting. I am simply saying when we praise God, when we rejoice in God; it's the Spirit of God that sustains us.

'*... for the joy of the Lord is your strength.*'
(Nehemiah 8:1)

For just a second, let's have another praise break! I need you to stop right there! Stop what you are doing. Turn the television off. Clear yourself of all distractions. No more pity parties. Throw out all the devil's invitations. Right now I command you to saturate the atmosphere with your praise. Shout hallelujah! Sing the songs of Zion. Be as David and encourage yourself in the Lord. The old saints used to say, 'When praises go up, blessings come down.' So I say, praise your way out. Put those hands together. Get up and stomp on the devil's head. Declare the victory. It's already yours! That's right praise your way happy! You need to praise, like you need your next breath. C'mon now, praise Him! It's what we do!

'*I will bless the Lord at all times: his praise shall continually be in my mouth.*' (Psalms 34:4)

Down through the years I have come to realize this one thing, that my blessing is directly connected to my praise. It is our duty, the Bible even says it's our reasonable service, to praise God and rejoice always. We owe it to God to bring Him our best praise! The way I look at it, when God looks at my praise it causes Him to bless me, for He knows my effort and He sees my tears. My praise causes the favor of God to rest upon me. It causes the blessings of God to overtake me.

'O clap your hands, all ye people; shout unto God with the voice of triumph.' (Psalms 47:1)

My praise is my weapon. It shields me. It encourages me. I must admit the Word is what keeps me but praise is what sustains me. Can you imagine going all week long trying to keep up with life's demands? There's work, school, the gym, coming home to cook, helping with homework, paying the bills, dealing with the kids and not have the joy of the Holy Ghost to sustain you? Even worse, can you imagine going to a dead or a dry church were the Spirit of God does not flow freely? Can you just picture it? No worship or limited praise? My God, my God!

There are some folks who are just like the Pharisee, who believe it doesn't take all of that. They cannot relate nor do they understand the purpose of all your hand clapping and feet stomping. They don't understand why you shout and sing like you do. Even more so, they sit bewildered scratching their heads wondering how you still have joy with all the hell you've gone through. I remember the mothers of the church would say,

'This joy that I have, the world didn't give it and the world can't take it away.' They want to know how you can smile and havoc is breaking loose in your life. They want to know the key to your happiness when life throws you a curve ball. Just let me make it plain. Their number one mistake is…we don't praise Him for what He does BUT because who He is! So, go ahead and tell them. When you couldn't bring yourself through, God brought you through.

> *'Bless the Lord, O my soul: and all that is within me, bless his holy name.'* (Psalms 103:1)

I regret absolutely nothing. My only wish is that I'd come to the knowledge of who Jesus is much sooner than I did. If I could be so bold as to say, I truly wish it hadn't taken even this long for me to accept this prophetic calling on my life. Truth is, I love being saved and sanctified. When I come into the sanctuary no one has to force me to clap my hands or get me to stand on my feet. I know what God has done for me. Whether I'm in the church or driving in the car, I know how to praise God. So you see you don't have to pump and prime me to exalt Him. I am capable of doing that all by myself. God is. He's worthy of the glory, worthy of the honor, and most definitely worthy of all the praise!

> *'Let everything that hath breath praise the Lord. Praise ye the Lord.'* (Psalms 150:6)

Somebody said, 'When I think of the goodness of Jesus and ALL He's done for me…my soul cries out *'hallelujah.'* I don't know about you but that just made me rejoice! When my mind goes back and I realize that God has kept me! He's kept me even from myself! Whew! Praising God brings me great joy. It comforts me. It sustains me. It strengthens me. I love the sound of praise: the tambourines when they rattle and the drums when they rumble. It's something supernatural about the saints praising God. Praise can set the atmosphere for deliverance. Sick bodies can be healed when there's praise. God can heal broken hearts during praise. Didn't you know? There's power in your praise!

People who really don't know or assume to know me, don't understand my praise. They hear my testimony of how God saved me at 16 years old and ask do I miss it. Do I miss what? is my question to them. Some even question if I feel I missed out on life because I got saved at an early age. My answer is no. If anything, Christ gave me life!

Hey, if you were looking for me to say what I could've or should've done before I got saved then you won't find it. At the end of the day I hold nothing against God. I love God. My heart yearns for Him. Again, I love being saved. He is and was the best thing that has ever happened in my life. Christ is the only thing that makes sense in my life. He is my peace. He is my joy. Glory to God! I rejoice in being saved and not just saved but saved for real. I don't know about you, but Jesus makes me happy!

'Rejoice in the Lord always: again I say rejoice.'
(Philippians 4:4)

Chapter 6: *Revelation & Appreciation*

Oh, my gosh! Wait one minute. Don't flip the page. I need to share this with you. I simply cannot believe it. Pinch me. My eyes are wide open, truly I can see. I can honestly see clearer now than I ever have seen before. In the Spirit, God has shown me just how this prophetic gift, even my anointing, will make room for me; the doors that will be opened, and the souls saved. If I say I am amazed, astonished, or even in awe would be the closest I come to conveying just how I feel.

Nevertheless, God showed me in the Spirit just how the pain and sorrow I have endured in this season will take my anointing to the next level. Again, God said to me, 'My glory is manifested in your tears.' I understand now that my pain will propel my anointing. It is my anointing that will stir this prophetic gift within me. Therefore, this gift will make room for me.

My sisters and brothers let me tell you in the Spirit that my jaw is dropped open and my mouth is gapping wide. Whew!

This revelation just blew my natural mind. My God! My God!

'For I reckon that the sufferings of this present time are not worthy to be compared with the glory which shall be revealed in us.' (Romans 8:18)

God surely knows that possessing this prophetic gift has definitely been a revelation of who I was born and always meant to be in Christ before the foundation of the world. Therefore, by no means do I take it lightly. God has made me privy to such a divine unveiling.

The very word *revelation* sends chills down my spine. Are you ready to talk about something being revealed? So, you say you need God to reveal His plans for your life to you? You ask God to show you a sign? My friend let me be the one to tell you, that you may not just see it or know it but you may experience it. Be wise in what it is you seek God for. Remember, He is a prayer-answering God!

Often times we want God to show us something we're unsure about yet we aren't prepared when He does. Let me paint a picture for you. Somewhere in the world, a woman is praying for God to show her if her husband still loves her and if his love is true. God reveals to her during prayer (add a bit of evidence) that her husband has been cheating all this time. Now she's angry with God. Why did she marry him she asks? Yet, she prayed for a revelation.

Better yet, imagine this…a businessman starts a new business venture. He asks God to show him a sign if his business is going to be a success. During Sunday service, the man of God prophesies warning and destruction to him. Instead of yielding to God and counting his losses he moves forward. Months later, he discovers that his business partner has been embezzling money. The business suffers and soon bottoms out. God gave prophetic revelation. He did His part as God. See, we expect God to come one way but God comes His own way. The prophet Isaiah told us that our ways are not God's ways and neither are our thoughts like God's.

Ever since I can remember I always wanted to be used of God. As a little girl I was completely in awe of the Glory of God. I was mesmerized by how it rested upon the saints. Please understand this, that the glory of God is not merely supernatural but also incomprehensible. You can't even begin to understand the ways of God!

'Hast thou not known? Hast thou not heard, that the everlasting God, the Lord, the Creator of the ends of the earth, faimteth not, neither is weary? There is no searching of his understanding.' (Isaiah 40:28)

We want the Glory of God but we don't want to bear the weight of the Glory. We want to be anointed and used by God but we don't want to go through anything. We don't want to suffer. We don't want to lose our friends. We don't want our feelings hurt. We attempt to avoid rejection. However, we want to feel God's glory. We want our ministries to take off. We pray for the favor of God to go before us. We go so far as to testify even, 'If nobody else will go then send me, Lord. I'll go.' Oh but when God begins to move we then find ourselves unprepared for the revelation. Let me say it plainly, my friend. We aren't prepared for tribulation.

One thing I've learned in this life is that as much as we despise tests and trials, heartache and pain, or the sorrows of this life; it is God who will cause the very hurt that you are going through to reveal His greatness to you.

As a young girl I suffered much abuse over the years. Sometimes the abuse was physical, verbal, or emotional and then there was the sexual abuse at the hands of family friends, family members, and even kids from school. Being young then I didn't know what to do with the hurt. I was afraid to tell my mother and father or anyone. So, I suffered in silence. I was a kid who was not sure what to do and where to go. That pain tormented me for years. I walked around smiling but on the inside I was broken. Nothing but the grace of God truly healed my heart. I appreciate God's comfort. One day as I was praying the Spirit of the Lord spoke to me, 'Why are you carrying something that can no longer hurt you?' I began to realize those chains are no longer binding me. I gave all the hurt, all the pain to God. It wasn't mine to bear. God delivered me. Right then God's healing caused me to forgive those who hurt me.

In the body of Christ sometimes abuse tends to be a discussion we pray about rather than talk about. Only when we are transparent in these sensitive areas can God deliver us from them and we can become truly free. Man of God and Woman of God listen to me, know that there's no shame in testifying how God is a Keeper, a Deliverer, a Healer! The enemy wants us to be silent and bottle it all in, walking in defeat and dying on the inside. Your testimony is a beacon of light to someone else who is in darkness. It is your God-given duty to reveal to others what God has revealed to you: deliverance, healing, and mercy. Here's the revelation; the enemy meant it for your bad but God used it for your good! Testify of the goodness of Jesus! Destroy the yoke of bondage. You are free in Christ. By His stripes you are healed. My God is a Deliverer! My God is a Defender! He's a Healer!

'But thanks be to God, which giveth us the victory through our Lord Jesus Christ.' (1 Corinthians 15:57)

I am not defeated! I encourage you, my sister or brother, to know that you are not defeated either! Our lives are not determined solely by what we have gone through. Repeat after me, 'I am NOT my past.' The enemy tries to hold our past against us to make us feel ashamed of what God has already delivered us from. The devil is a lie! Listen, I understand and I know the hurt you feel seems to be unfair. I know the betrayal you felt then has cut real deep. I even know how you have wrestled with that 'thing' and even those bad decisions that followed it. Nevertheless you made it! Understand and know that even in our suffering Christ is glorified.

I stand boldly when I say to you that I refuse to allow the enemy to even think what happened to me as a child will be a smudge on my destiny or defer my anointing.

'But the God of all grace, who hath called us unto his eternal glory by Christ Jesus, after that ye have suffered

a while, make you perfect, stablish, strengthen, settle you.' (1Peter 5:10)

My friend, it'll be the very storm you want to run from that God will reveal the hidden things to you. He'll even reveal the greatness that lies dormant in you. I can attest; for God knows I am a witness.

I can recall the time when my husband decided to be a part of another ministry other than the rest of the family. At first my heart was shattered within me. I will admit. At the time I did not understand just why this type of pain would happen to me, let alone so openly…where everyone knew. See, it is one thing to go through it in private but when God allows what you're going through to be made public, that is another matter. They said my house was divided. My family's anguish was open to all who had an opinion even in the church. There were those who shared with me their callous remarks. I would be lying to say those remarks didn't sting a little. Even so, God strategically placed some of the saints in my life to pour their love and encouragement into me. Somebody prayed for me. They told me to keep trusting God and no matter what, continue to stand on the promises of God. I did just that.

Truth be told, I wanted to crawl within myself and hide from folks; at times that even meant the church. Every Sunday morning in the car, my children would ask why their father wasn't going to church with us until one day they just stopped asking. As much as I wanted to burst into tears and allow my emotions to rule, I stayed in the Spirit and told them to keep praying for their father. No doubt I wanted to run from this storm. In fact, I tried to elude it as much as I could. Yet, it wasn't going anywhere anytime soon.

One day, as I was lying on my face praying and fasting, crying to God about this storm and every other, the Spirit of the Lord spoke to my spirit and said, 'You're just going to have to go through this.' Simple as that. There was no magic door with an exit sign. There was no *abracadabra*. God let me know right at that moment that the only way I was going to come out was if I went through.

In the beginning of this thing, I felt as if I was walking around in a trance. At the time I was too focused on it and not focused enough on God. Nevertheless, I thank God for His grace. I can't exactly explain it to you, but over time the more that storm brewed the more I prayed and eventually it became just another test. Did it hurt? Yes, but it didn't hold the same power over me as it once did. God encouraged me. The Spirit of the Lord strengthened me. The Word of God spoke life back into me. God renewed my mind. He reminded me there is purpose even in my pain. My God! My God! Talk about a revelation!

'Unless thy law had been my delights, I should then have perished in mine afflictions.' (Psalms 119: 92)

It's peculiar really. After all the rain, God is gracious enough to let us see the bright sunshine. Hear me when I say that with every trial, every test, every heartache, and every disappointment comes revelation. I know it hurts right now...BUT GOD! You survived! You made it! The storms of life may come and the winds may blow yet one thing I learned is that I am nothing without God. After all I've been through I've learned to appreciate God in the good times and in the bad times. The storm is only temporary. My God is a Deliverer.

'I will bless the Lord at all times; his praise shall continually be in my mouth.' (Psalms 34:1)

I caution you to take heed my friend. Often times we never really learn to appreciate something until it's gone or it's threatened. So it was when I accepted this prophetic calling. For so long I tried to hide from God. I foolishly tried to convince myself things weren't quite what they were; that God wasn't calling me. I erroneously believed I was already doing all that God called me to do. It never occurred to me then that my destiny was greater than I could ever imagine, that the test and trials I was going through were preparing me for the next level in God.

Catch this revelation; your promotion comes from the fire! You better believe it! There comes a time when tears will no longer suffice. I am not telling you that you can't cry sometimes. No, I am not saying that. What I am saying is if you have to cry then go ahead and shed a few tears. However, you must likewise arm yourselves to fight and to keep fighting. I've come to understand this one thing in the Spirit, the more the enemy fights against me then the more I war in the Spirit. The more I praise God! Embrace the warrior that's within you. God has given us this revelation way before the battle even began. We always win! We always come out on top. We are destined to be great! I admonish you to appreciate the mantle God has entrusted you with just as Elijah did Elisha. For Jesus tells us in Matthew 22:14, '*For many are called, but few are chosen.*' God chose YOU!   Everyone is not equipped to handle the weight of the Glory but YOU ARE. So walk in grace. Fight with purpose! Appreciate the champion in you!

Chapter 7: *Prophecy Unleashed*

My God! My God! I can see in the Spirit the barriers all around me breaking piece by piece, brick by brick and wall by wall. Lord knows I've tried. I have tried my best to contain it. I even tried to conceal it, to restrain it. Yet the Spirit of the Living God spoke to me and said, 'Let go!' Therefore in divine obedience to His voice, I released my grasp and just like lightning bolting out of the heavens in the midst of a thunderstorm, this prophetic gift that I tried to elude for so long suddenly became unleashed.

> *'Then I said, I will not make mention of him, nor speak any more in his name. But his Word was in mine heart as a burning fire shut up in my bones, and I was weary with forbearing, and I would not stay.'* (Jeremiah 20:9)

Have you ever cooked something in a pot and placed the lid on it but no matter how much you'd tried turning the heat down, the contents within it just bubbled? In the beginning the contents gently seeps over the lid. The longer the pot is over the heat, it begins to bubble more…even gargle. Eventually, the lid is useless. The contents start spilling and flowing effortlessly. So it has been with this prophetic calling over my life. From the time I open my mouth, I am reminded of the call to speak only when God says speak.

Let me set the record straight. This prophetic calling on my life wasn't spoken to me by some preacher or even given to me by the laying on of hands. No, God Himself bestowed this divine gift upon me. It's simply a result of having a discipline and consecrated life before Him. This means much prayer and not your microwave popcorn prayer but fervent in prayer, fasting, and reading His Word. I had to learn to die to myself. Spiritually, this flesh had to die. I had to die to MY plans, MY thoughts, MY opinions, MY ways, MY feelings, and MY attitude. Yes, you read correctly. We must even die to our own attitudes. Saints, if you haven't done so already, you need to get there quick, fast, and in a hurry. Die to your bad temper, die to petty ways, let go of that haughty spirit, and that lying tongue. No more excuses! Deny yourselves!!

'Then said Jesus unto his disciples, If any man will come after me, let him deny himself, and take up his cross, and follow me.' (Matthew 16:24)

Know that God is ever merciful. He is patient and just. The Bible tells us in Lamentations 3:22,

'It is of the Lord's mercies that we are not consumed,

because his compassion fail not.'

He allows us to come to Him just as we are. So come. No excuses. Here's your coming to Jesus moment. Ta-da! Let Jesus unleash the sin in your life and come. If you are a drug dealer then come. If you are a liar, then come on. Let the homosexual, the murderer, the backslider, and even the lying prophet now come. One thing is undisputed; God is holy. You may come to him wretched and full of sin. You can be raggedy, dirty, even the black sheep; however when the power of a Holy God is unleashed in your life He causes all things to be new.

'Therefore if any man be in Christ, he is a new creature: old things are passed away; behold, all things are become new.' (1 Corinthians 5:17)

Listen, if you plan to be anything in the Body of Christ then you must be willing to die to yourself and live a purified and sanctified life. As I walk down memory lane I recall the moments when those around me believed I always did too much when it came to Holiness. Some of my peers thought of me as odd because at my age I never had a drink. I didn't club at all. In high school some of the kids would laugh and mock me for wearing long skirts. Even some of my family said it wasn't necessary to go from service to service, giving and sowing. Their mistake was in thinking that my efforts, my dedication, my loyalty was to man. Wrong! My heart belonged to God. True believers seek after the ways and the presence of God by any means necessary. We understand that our very existence, our next blessing, our anointing is divinely connected to God. To know Him is to love Him.

'For in him we live, and move, and have our being...'
(Acts 17:28)

See, the problem is that you have a lot of people in the church but not enough people in Christ. He seeks to have an intimate relationship with his children. Beware of those who will preach, teach, and tell you otherwise. Folks will knowingly walk sloppy in this Christian race and then try to pollute your spirit and taint your heart. Their lives don't line up with the Word of God therefore they will try to convince you to have low standards in Holiness as well. Understand this, you can come to church, you can have a title and a pulpit to stand be-hind, you may even have a gift but still lack the anointing. If that's you, then who are you fooling? His expectations are clear. Ask yourself this question: Do I favor God? Does my life reflect Christ? Jesus said,

'My sheep hear my voice, and I know them, and they follow me.' (John 10:27)

Friends, allow me to give you a nugget of wisdom. God is not the author of confusion. Watch for those who say one thing with their mouths and mean another in their hearts. It may even be those close to you. They will admonish you, encourage you, and support you. They'll cheer you on for all the weight you've lost. They'll help you build your business and pat you on the back as you plan to go back to school. Yet when you make the effort to live righteously then it's a problem. It becomes an issue of you not spending enough time, no fun to be around, and just too serious. If what I said applies to you then God has called you to lift up a standard of holiness far above the rest. He wants to raise you up in the midst of a crowd and set you as one of His own. There's an assignment over your life.

> *'For many are called, but few are chosen.'* (Matthew 22:14)

See, it took me a while to get here but I made it! I've come through the storm and the rain. For so long I prayed for God to stop the rain. (It really felt like a monsoon). It was one day when I was laying on my face fasting and praying that God revealed to me that even after the rain there is growth. Catch the revelation!

Man and woman of God of The Most High, let me speak prophetically to your heart. You must learn to stop asking God to work this out, work that out, stop this, stop that, deliver me from this, deliver me from that. Know that God is working it out on your behalf even if you can't see it with your natural eyes. Your change may not come the way you want it to but either way God will get the glory if you just go through. Don't cast off what God has ordained.

I'm not telling you something that I didn't have to understand first myself. The Spirit of the Living God spoke to me clearly one day during prayer. It's in the rain, it's through the pain, the test, and the season of heartache that I am rebirthing you, and unleashing my prophetic anointing in you.

Allow me to be transparent my friend. When I wanted to quit, when I wanted to give up, when I cried out Lord this seems to be just too much and I wanted to throw in the towel…the anointing over my life would not allow it. This prophetic call was ordained upon my life before the moment my father met my mother. God birthed purpose in me way before my momma even gave natural birth to me, before I could take my first breath. Therefore, I learned and now understand the significance of my anointing. The greater God uses me, the greater the enemy presses me, and then even greater is the prophetic anointing that rests upon me. So, in order to unleash this prophetic gift I must first humble myself under the mighty hand of God. I must yield to the will of God…not for my glory but to God be the glory! If I learned anything by now it's that my help, my strength, my deliverance did not manifest until I yielded my will to God!

'Saying, Father, if thou be willing, remove this cup from me: nevertheless not my will, but thine, be done.'
(Luke 22:42)

Listen now as I impart this prophetic word into your life. This is not the season nor the time to shy away from the process. Rise up and be courageous! The God you serve is unleashing a new anointing through you right now. I know it's been hard and at times you didn't always understand it. Step into this new level with grace. The very storms you've been through have brought you to this pivotal moment. You were made for this! God is pushing you from behind the veil and unleashing such an anointing that will stir the very gift that's within you to prepare you. So, brace yourself! It's here!

I speak to that seed in your belly that was planted so long ago in faith. I speak to that prophetic seed that holds the promises of God. It's that seed of dreams, that seed of prayer, that seed of hope, that consecrated seed of divine faith. Man and Woman of God, I know you didn't think you would make it to see it. At times things looked as if they could not get any worse. Yet you didn't give up! The Spirt of the Lord is upon me to tell you that that very seed is sprouting up in your life even now. God will keep His promises. For the abundance of the latter rain is about to be made manifest for all to see even those who mocked you, ridiculed you, and abandoned you for planting, for yet hoping, for yet believing. Unleash your harvest!

> '*And I will restore to you the years that the locust hath eaten, the cankerworm, and the caterpillar, and the palmerworm, my great army which I sent among you. And ye shall eat in plenty, and be satisfied, and praise the name of the Lord your God that hath dealt wondrously with you: and my people shall never be ashamed.*' (Joel 2:25-26)

For so long, I tried to hide from this level of anointing. I didn't understand then, what I know now. I was created for this! I can see the favor of God shifting in me and moving me to the next level in the Spirit realm. Isn't this amazing about

God; how what took others a lifetime to achieve, God would unlock and unleash within you in a matter of moments? My God! My God! I am a living testimony! Just let go and let God! The Spirit of the Lord says, while you are enjoying this season, I will be preparing greater for you in the next season. God says, you're going to have to make room for the NEW. He's doing a NEW thing! If only you remain in me and be obedient then what's coming is better than what's been.

'Behold, I will do a new thing; now it shall spring forth; shall ye not know it? I will even make a way in the wilderness, and rivers in the desert.' (Isaiah 43:19)

There are times in your life were you will have to prophesy over your own self! Go ahead and prophesy over your marriage and over your children. Prophesy over your ministry, over your health, over your business, over your finances, and over all that God has given you dominion over. Speak it! Stop waiting for somebody to come into your life to speak a word of faith. You must learn to speak the Words of Life yourself! God has given you the very power to have what you say. Stop asking for peace. Command it! If you're crazy enough to believe it, then God is crazy (radical) enough to do it! If you have the Holy Ghost then you have the power! Use it. Tap into the power source! God has given you Divine authority. Unlock the next level in God. Don't pull back! Today is your day and now is your moment! Go ahead now. Unleash the Glory of God into the very atmosphere. God gave you possession of it…now UNLEASH it!

Chapter 8: *Unfeigned Faith*

Brace yourself! One, two, three…now jump! Ah, that's it; now jump by faith! C'mon, now. See, where I am going in God. I'm running and I'm leaping over mountains by faith. I am running earnestly with all the strength that's in me in the Spirit. In this season in my life if I have to run, that's what I'll do. If I have to leap, jump, roll, swim, fly, dance then that's just what I'm willing to do. Where ever and whenever my faith says go, just know that I am going.

'Beloved, when I gave all diligence to write unto you of the common salvation, it was needful for me to write unto you, and exhort you that ye should earnestly contend for the faith which was once delivered unto the saints.' (Jude 1:3)

My mind recalls when the Apostle Paul charged Timothy

to continue in the faith, charging him to stir up the gift and how astonished he was seeing the unfeigned faith in Timothy. (2 Timothy 2:1) This is the same faith he saw in Timothy's grandmother, Lois, and mother, Eunice. I longed for God to see the same unfeigned faith in me. Unfeigned faith isn't just your textbook version of faith. It's extraordinary faith, sincere faith. When I close my eyes, I can only imagine all the other apostles and servants of the Lord that Paul came across during his life-time. He crossed paths with so many of God's people. Paul spent time with Mark, Barnabus, even the Apostle Peter…and Jesus gave him the keys to the kingdom. Nevertheless, it was Timothy whose faith outshined all the others. From my heart I pray, God see my sincerity, my genuineness, and my honesty. I pray, Lord see the true, unforced, real heartfelt faith in me, your daughter, Natisha, just as Paul saw in your servant, Timothy.

I have purposed in my heart to keep running for God…whatever it takes…by faith. I must keep pressing, keep singing, keep praising and yes, keep prophesying. Whatever it takes to move forward in God because I can't and I won't go back! Man and woman of God there's too much ahead of you. Look with your spiritual eyes. If truth be told we have wasted enough time; wasted time on simple things. We've wasted time on meaningless and careless things in this life that don't birth purpose. My friend, I don't know about you and where you stand with God but I've come to this one conclusion; we are in the fight of our lives. Consider this your public service an-nouncement. If you don't have the faith to push yourself through then you just might faint. I don't know about you but I come too far in God to just lose all faith in Him and faint now. There's greatness ahead.

It's out of the deepest parts of my heart, when I say to you, you MUST have faith. It's essential to every believer. Well, Prophetess, what is faith? The Bible tells us,

> *'Now faith is the substance of things hoped for, the evidence of things not seen.'* (Hebrews 11:1)

Faith is believing and yet not seeing. Faith is believing God to hold true to His promises even when you've yet to see them come to pass. Faith is giving God your ten percent out of love and out of obedience to the Word even though the light bill is sitting on the table. Faith is trusting God to be a healer even though you may have pain aching in your body. Can I ask you this question? Whose report will you believe? My faith tells me God is a provider. He's Jehovah Jireh. My faith tells me He's a Balm in Gilead and that He's the Great Physician. My faith says God is All in all.

You must understand that the God we serve is ever faithful, not just sometimes but all the time. Great is Thy faithfulness! He cannot lie and neither can His word return to Him void. He will do just what He said He would do. If He spoke it, shall He not do it? God is not like man. He does not speak just for the fancy of it or better yet to hear Himself talk. He could if He wanted to because He's God. But no, my friend, this is not the case over your life. Know that when God speaks, He speak purpose to those promises. So, let me help you understand this clearly. All you need to activate those promises of God in your life is faith! He moves according to our faith. Where is your faith? Do you have radical faith? Can your faith stand? While you examine your heart man and woman of God, I challenge you further to examine your faith. Faith is not your feelings!

Know that having faith in God, and I mean real faith, the faith that Paul saw in Timothy… will always be tried in the fire. What's the 'fire'? It's tests and trials, trials and tribulations. See, only when our faith is tried and tested can it be proven really unfeigned. Then and only then can we then call our faith sincere, real or even genuine.

Understand, when a refiner tests gold for its authenticity it is then put in the fire to see its true value. He must test it over and over again to be certain that the gold he is refining is purified. The more it's purified, the greater its worth. So it is with our faith. God is seeing just how well we stand under pressure. Will we buckle? Will we give in? Can we stand? It's in the fire that we find strength. It's in the fire that we are delivered. My brothers and sisters it is in the fire that we are purified. Don't be mistaken. Faith that's not tried is not faith at all. Just like the cubic zirconia or costume jewelry…it's fake.

> *'That the trial of your faith, being much more precious than of gold that perisheth, though it be tried with fire, might be found unto praise and honor and glory at the appearing of Jesus Christ.'* (1 Peter 1:7)

See, some of us like to believe that though we go through it's always the devil on our backs. I somewhat agree. The Bible tells us that he's our adversary. He walks about seeking whom he may devour. Yet I beg this one time to differ friend. If you disagree, let's just agree to disagree. However, there are times when God has to try us…to refine us in the fire to work some things out of us. You know? Those things, those habits, and those unpleasing ways…the list goes on. So, how effective can we be if we are still struggling or still tripping up over what Jesus called 'the little foxes'? How can we move to the next level in God and still be dragging baggage behind us? How effective will I be if I preached Jesus is a Deliverer but I'm not delivered? Here's the golden answer…not effective enough.

I don't care how long you've been saved. It's not a matter of how long you've been going to church. Going through tests and trials doesn't always feel good. Often times as children of God, in this life we face much pain and heartache. It is I who have learned this all too well as I moved to the next level in God into the prophetic. There were several days that I had to fight back the tears. Still, I had to speak to my own self. I had to speak to the faith that was in me. As I ministered to others, God ministered to me. I wanted and needed God to come see about me. Oh yes, my faith was tried.

'Many are the afflictions of the righteous: but the Lord delivereth him out of them all.' (Psalms 34:19)

When the doctors told us that my father had colon cancer and that surgery was immediate, instead of going berserk or pacing the floor I did quite the opposite. I had to reach way deep down on the inside past all the hurt, past my emotions, and grab a hold of some radical faith. Having faith in God was not an option but a requirement!

After losing our first home in 2011 to foreclosure we started renting houses for our family thereafter. Now, if anybody has had to rent a home then they know it is more costly than owning your own home. Still folks had their comments and their questions. They wondered how our home went into foreclosure. Family asked us if we could even afford our bills. See, despite how I may have felt at the present time or regardless of the situations of life, one thing I understood is that things may come and things may go. Yet I still had my faith. So, we prayed. We looked beyond where we were at and trusted God. We took that great big ol leap of faith almost 7 years later! Yes we did. We did it! Better yet, God did it! We bought our second home with 3 bedrooms, 2 full baths, a fireplace, all brand new stainless steel appliances, new floors, new windows, large backyard with a swing set included. Don't tell me what God won't do! Faith moves God.

Let me encourage you man and woman of God for just a moment. Stop looking at your credit score. Income doesn't factor when God is blessing. Just stop for a moment. Stop paying attention to your human reason and your carnal knowledge. The God we serve is supernatural. I am not telling you to be unwise or do anything ridiculous. What I am encouraging you to do is…take that ridiculous faith and trust a wise God.

'But ye, beloved, building up yourselves on your most holy faith, praying in the Holy Ghost…To the only wise God our Saviour, be glory and majesty, dominion and power, both now and ever, Amen.' (Jude 1:20 & 25)

When the doctors told me the probability of me having another child was slim to none, I admit the news didn't sound good. Right there my husband and I could've given up on trying. There were even those who tried to persuade us that we should be grateful for having our two daughters. They said just be satisfied. The 'baby fever' will pass. Thanks be unto God, who giveth us the victory! I prayed. I fasted. There were times I cried. Still, we petitioned God for a son. I know what faith will do. The saints laid hands on me and by the end of the year I was pregnant. On February 19, 2016 we welcomed our baby boy into the world.

Let me admonish you, child of God, ignore the naysayers and all the Doubting Thomas's. Stop allowing yourself to get distracted by what you see. You must learn to speak faith. Speak it until you see it, until it manifests. Speak it into the very atmosphere. Hold fast to your faith! Don't let others shake your faith. Your faith is precious. It will take you where others only wish they could go.

The remarkable thing about faith is that it will cause you to walk in your authority. It will cause you to speak to the mountains in your life and command them to be removed. Faith will cause the giants in your life to fall. Faith…no ordinary faith but unfeigned faith will cause you to speak things into existence, plans into motion and dreams into reality.

I write to encourage you. Hold fast to your faith! Put your faith into action. God gave you a business plan. Stop dreaming about it and start preparing for it. If God strengthened you to run the next 5K marathon then don't look at others and allow your faith to be shaken. No, lace those shoes up and register for that race. Man of God, if God said branch out and gave you instructions to start your own church then put that faith to work and write the vision and make it plain. Your faith moves God when you put it into action. Trust God. He sees the blood, sweat, and tears you have labored just to keep moving forward. He's neither blind nor ignorant. He sees and He knows…and yes, He cares. Motion your faith! Activate your faith! Faith your way through! Yes, I said it. Just like that too. You know the funny thing is, once you obtained faith…you must fight to keep it. So, again, faith your way through.

'But will thou know, O vain man, that faith without works is dead,' (James 2:20)

You can spend the whole day long saying that you have faith; in fact, until you are blue in the face. You can buy the T-shirt and the bumper sticker. Still, if there's no works, no actions, or no deeds to go along with it…then I hate to spill the beans. Your faith isn't real faith. It's just empty talk and nothing more. Romans 10:17 tell us,

'So then faith cometh by hearing and hearing by the word of God.'

Let me ask you this one question. How can you have faith if you never heard or read the word of God? Where is your faith, if you say to yourself *I don't have to listen to a preacher? I don't have to go to church. I can read the Bible myself.*

Where is your faith? How did you then obtain it? Is it sustainable? Can your faith stand? Will it carry you through or is it here today and gone tomorrow? Does your faith change as the wind blows?

My heart is transparent before you when I say it took me stepping out on faith to even write these very words to you, to put my life on paper. It took even more faith for me to operate and to walk in the prophetic. Yes, I know what the Bible tells me to do. I know that God is the Author and Finisher of our faith. Yet it took a greater leap of faith on my part to solely put my trust in God and not in myself, not in my emotions and definitely not in what I can see. I don't care what folks may say. Perception isn't everything. Faith doesn't require you to have 20/20 vision. God didn't ask you to read all the letters or numbers on the ophthalmologist board. Nope. See, faith has nothing to do with your human eyesight. You have to believe first and see later.

'*For we walk by faith, not by sight.*' (2 Corinthians 5:7)

I've come a long way in God. Truth be told, yes, there were times when my faith waivered. There were times during this nineteen-year journey when I should have stayed focused and I didn't. My unbelief almost cost me not only my next blessing but also my anointing. If we could just be honest we would save ourselves a lifetime of disappointment and in the process encourage someone else along the way. You don't have to tell on yourselves. I am mature enough to be honest and real before God, myself. This is me in my purest form. So, it's no secret that I have struggled with this prophetic gift. First, my struggle was to understand it, accepting it, and then I found myself running from it. My God. My God. My anointing followed me like a large cloud moving overhead. My faith was truly being tested. In the early years in God I echoed the words 'I love God' and 'God is everything.' Nevertheless, God wanted to know just how much I truly loved Him. Was it all talk? My faith was on the line.

'But without faith it is impossible to please him: for he that cometh to God must believe that he is, and that he is a rewarder of them that diligently seek him,' (Hebrews 11:6)

Walking by faith through those spiritual doors, and watching the gift of prophesy being unleashed in my life has definitely been a journey of faith. It has aggressively seized every part of my very being. See, once I got pass the obstacles and the distractions in my way, then I could move forward in my gift. Even then I had to get pass the obstacles of fear, hurt, unbelief, and even the obstacle of SELF. Then, operating in the prophetic no longer was a challenge but an honor. Therefore, I count myself as the Apostle Paul who says,

'And I thank Christ Jesus our Lord, who hath enabled me, for that he counted me faithful, putting me into ministry.' (1 Timothy 1:12)

Regardless of what may or may not have happened in my

life, at the end of the day I just want to please God. It may sound a bit brash but in the grand scheme of things nothing else matters. I passed those tests. I've fought, battled and it may have taken me awhile but I won. I declare in Jesus' name that I've got the victory!

'But thanks be unto God who gives us the victory through our Lord Jesus Christ,' (1 Corinthians 15:57)

While I expose my heart before you and make myself available to God, I don't have any time to worry about who can or cannot recognize the gift that's in me. One thing I have learned through manifold trials and tests, I don't have to prove my gift or my anointing to anyone but God…and He's the one who called me! I've been there and done that. God knows me. He knows my faith and trust in Him. He knows everything there is to know about me. So, yeah, go ahead; He knows all about my past. Yep, he surely knows where my faith stands. Go ahead and whisper all the times I've stumbled and cradled unbelief when I should've let it go. Tell about the times I cried and I should have dried my eyes and trusted God…because yep, he knows that too. Let me let you in on my secret; which is really no secret at all. My faith, my anointing, my prophetic gift…that's in God!

Listen, man of God and woman of God, you better know for sure that if God called you and equipped you then there's no explanation or story needed behind it to satisfy people. People will never be satisfied, whether you have faith or not. So, put your faith in God. People are like seasons. They come and they go. I don't care what your title is. You don't have to be a prophet or a bishop to know that I am talking to you. Search the scriptures. Know who you are in God and that you fit in His kingdom.

'Faithful is he that calleth you, who also will do it,' (1 Thessalonians 5:24)

When I flip through the pages of this thing called life and I examine my walk in God on this Christian journey…I thank God for His grace and mercy. I can truly see maturity and the hand of God upon me. Even more so, I can see how faith has carried me through; not just the good times but even in those bad times.

If you don't remember anything else, please remember this, faith moves God. Repeat after me. 'My faith moves God.' Now, take that same crazy, ridiculous, don't-make-no sense faith you have in God and run like the wind! Drop the weights! What's the weight you may ask? Drop those things that will hinder your faith. Drop all the distractions, the disappointments, the fear, the past…drop the unbelief. C'mon now! Stop procrastinating. No more excuses. All it takes is one big leap. Go ahead and try it. You can do it! All it takes is a little faith! You got this! God's got you! Soar!!

'For by thee I have run through a troop; and by my God have I leaped over a wall.' (Psalms 18:29)

Chapter 9: *A True Prophet*

Hear ye! Hear ye! Ladies and gentlemen, boys and girls, please gather around. Come and see this daring anomaly; the main attraction of this age! Come and see this bold false prophet parading in a preacher's robe. Caution! Beware of his cunning lies and devious tricks! He can fool millions with only an illusion.

If a prophet came into your presence or walked into your sanctuary holding a sign or wearing a T-shirt that read 'FALSE PROPHET' then a majority of you would undoubtedly avoid him or her at all cost. Nor would you believe the words that they spoke. Why? It's simply because the truth would be obvious. The words they speak bear absolutely no truth to stand on. Their words do not line up with the Word of God. So, they are anti-God, therefore anti-Christ.

'Beloved, believe not every spirit, but try the spirits whether they are of God: because many false prophets

are gone into the world...' (1 John 4:1)

Yet today the people of God have been rocked to sleep by these lying wonders and wolves in sheep's clothing. Wake up Men of God! Wake up Women of God! They have perfected their craft of cunningness by speaking big fancy words before large audiences and congregations. They lie while performing wonders to disguise their deception. Erroneously many leaders have opened the church doors and have allowed them to operate freely under false pretenses and no real anointing. This is why people of God that I say and I say again, we MUST stay awake! We MUST be alert!

'Be sober, be vigilant; because your adversary the devil, as a roaring lion, walketh about, seeking whom he may devour.' (1 Peter 5:8)

If we are not praying and if we are not careful, we would join in with the millions of others who dangerously and without wisdom flocked from East to West, from L.A. to New York, and anywhere in between just to hear a lie. They do not have a 'Word from Heaven.' God did not send them. They intentionally lie and the truth isn't in them. They cause division, chaos, murmuring, and rebellion in the House of God. Nevertheless, because they have ten thousand followers on social media, a mega ministry, and a name to light the marquee we deem them anointed and called of God. The lies they tell! Listen to me carefully with your spiritual ears. The Body of Christ must learn to follow the anointing and the not the illusion of it! It's the anointing that destroys the yoke.

'Then the Lord said unto me, The prophets prophesy lies in my name: I sent them not, neither have I commanded them, neither spake unto them: they prophesy unto you a false vision and divination, and a thing of nought, and the deceit of their heart.' (Jeremiah 14:14)

Stop for just a moment! I want you to participate in a little exercise with me. No, not jumping jacks and cartwheels. It's just a brief spiritual exercise. I want you to think of ten prophets that you know of, either locally or renowned. Now of those ten, how many do you know have an honest report? How many are truly saved? I'm talking about being saved for real. How many have the Holy Ghost? If for but a moment we can take our eyes off titles and stop looking at the powers and wonders that they do and truly look at their lifestyle then we would be better off. Understand this, people of God, we are no longer living in the last days but in the last hours.

'¹This know also, that in the last days perilous times shall come. ²For men shall be lovers of their own selves, covetous, boasters, proud, blasphemers, disobedient to parents, unthankful, unholy, ³Without natural affection, trucebreakers, false accusers, incontinent, fierce, despisers of those that are good, ⁴Traitors, heady, highminded, lovers of pleasures more than lovers of God; ⁵Having a form of godliness, but denying the power thereof: from such turn away.' (2 Timothy

3:1-5)

How can a prophet call him or herself 'called of God' and not know how to show love, especially to the Household of Faith? In all the visions that we see and all the tongues that we speak we ought to have mastered love; if in fact we are TRUE prophets at all. You can't pick and choose who of God's children gets to receive it. This truth applies to not only prophets but also to all us Children of God. I myself have a responsibility not only to God but also to my anointing as well…to live the life I prophesy about.

'And though I have the gift of prophecy, and understand all mysteries, and all knowledge; and though I have all faith, so that I can remove mountains, and have not charity, I am nothing.' (1 Corinthians 13:2)

Today, everybody in the church wants to be either gifted and/or anointed. If you are a prophet or declare yourself gifted or called of God in ANY office apply these questions to YOU (and not to your neighbor). Does my lifestyle reflect my calling? What does my character say about my gift? Do I exemplify a purified life? Do I have the characteristics of Christ? Do I favor God? The sad reality is many folks rather chase titles then chase God. There's a big problem with that. We have a pandemic on our hands. Use your spiritual eyes now and see.

Fast forward to today's generation and everyone either wants to be a prophet or everyone is running to hear from one. Lord have mercy! Although I remember a time growing up in

Holiness when if there was a prophet in the sanctuary, you prayed the prophet didn't call you out or call you forward. Be honest, people of God. You were too worried that the prophet would expose your mess and tell you to repent; talk about true prophets. Growing up in Christ, I remember the true prophets didn't patty-cake with the saints at the altar. If you were playing church, fornicating or sinning then they would order that foul spirit to be loose and command you to be saved for real. There wasn't any gray, only black and white. Again, I'm talking about true prophets. I can hear you loud and clear. Please don't misunderstand me. There are true prophets who also perform miracles, who also prophesy blessings of prosperity and wealth. See, true prophets speak truth at all times; whether that truth be divine blessings or godly correction. It's still TRUTH.

Church, let us just accept accountability for our part. Let us repent for turning a blind eye and compromising when we should have been rebuking and taking a stand for Holiness. Yeah, I hear you. It's not your fault. You didn't do anything...yeah, yeah, yeah. That's the problem as well. We didn't do ANYTHING. We gave these false prophets a platform all because they could draw numbers. We allowed our members to go to their revivals because 'at least they're going to church.' Here it is, that we have true prophets and prophetesses, men and women of God in our own churches and still we run to pay big money for a lie across town. My God! My God! The travesty!! These lying wonders have ONLY a form of godliness! It is nothing but an imitation, a copycat, and a decoy. They operate in the spirit of familiarity, which is the spirit of witchcraft, and call it prophecy. Lies! They are unclean spirits sinning and call themselves prophets of God; more like prophets of Baal. Amen, somebody!

> *'But there were false prophets also among the people, even as there shall be false teachers among you, who privily shall bring in damnable heresies, even denying the Lord that brought them, and bring upon themselves swift destruction.'* (2 Peter 2: 1)

Where are the TRUE prophets who will choose Holiness and not the crowds?! Where are the TRUE prophets who will choose salvation and not the money, not the titles, and not the fame?! Where are the TRUE prophets who will choose the anointing and not their image? Where are the TRUE prophets who will stand and choose to love God and not merely themselves?!

> *'But made himself of no reputation, and took upon him the form of a servant, and was made in the likeness of men...'* (Philippians 2:7)

When some people hear the word prophet it's often associated with foretelling the unknown. Yet a true prophet will confirm what God has already told or shown you when you are in right relation with God. We're not magicians or wizards. There's no abracadabra or hocus pocus and poof there it is. God doesn't work like that. Understand this my friend, the prophet can prophesy God's blessings over your life and speak into your life new houses, land, new businesses, healings and even miracles. According to thy faith be it done unto you. However, if you don't have the faith to believe it, then you'll never receive it. It's just that simple. See, the prophet can prophesy to the very atmosphere and God may even show them in your next season that you will be surrounded by divine favor; but the prophetic shift is according to YOUR faith!

'That your faith should not stand in the wisdom of men, but in the power of God.' (1 Corinthians 2:5)

There are those of you who may pose the question, 'Prophetess Wilson, how do you know when God has called you to the office of prophet? How do I know if I have the gift of prophesy? How do I know one to be a TRUE prophet?' Firstly, Man or Woman of God, if you profess to be called to this level of anointing, I caution you not to take it lightly by any means. Consider your calling. Consider the charge. For myself, God spoke to my spirit and elevated me to the office of a prophet at a young age and placed within me the gift to prophesy. Therefore, I count it an honor to serve God in this capacity and to speak before God's people. For I recognize it's no goodness of my own. I did nothing to earn it. It is a gift from God.

'¹⁰To another the working of miracles; to another prophecy; to another discerning of spirits; to another divers kinds of tongues; to another the interpretation of tongues: ¹¹But all these worketh that one and the self-

same Spirit, dividing to every man severally as he will.'
(1 Corinthians 12:10-11)

One thing I have learned down through the years and I stand on this principle fact. God gets all the glory in everything I do and all that I am. A true prophet doesn't have to broadcast to the world the prophetic calling upon their life. We understand that all power belongs to God. It's never about us.

'God hath spoken once; twice have I heard this; that power belongeth unto God.' (Psalms 62:11)

If I walk into a room full of church people and they say Minister Wilson or Evangelist Wilson or better yet, Sister Tish rather than Prophetess Wilson, my feathers aren't ruffled at all. Why? You see because at the end of the day it's only a title and not my anointing. It's not my calling that's overlooked. I know how to humble myself.

Now let's just be honest. Respect is one thing and giving honor where honor is due is another. Still, all the same, I refuse to come out of the Spirit or be lifted up high in pride because of a title or because Brother Bob and Sister Sally didn't recognize the calling upon my life. It's not that serious to me. Truth is, once we (the Body of Christ) can get pass titles then we can focus more on the true commission by which Christ called us.

Man of God, Woman of God listen to me carefully for a moment. I will say this and I leave it here. If they NEVER acknowledge you, if they claim to not know or see the elevation that God is doing in you then my advice is that you keep pushing. You keep on preaching, keep singing, keep prophesy-ing, keep praying and remain continuously before God. At the end of the day your character speaks volumes. Never forget that God gets all the glory…not you. Still, I promise you this, that the same gift that they tried to overlook will be the same gift that God will use to thrust you forward into your destiny. So trust me. You don't have to worry about a thing. Believe it or not they see the greatness in you, for God has favored you.

'A man's gift maketh room for him, and bringeth him before great men.' (Proverbs 18:16)

Allowing God to unleash this prophetic gift in my life and me yielding to it has definitely opened my eyes that much more in the Spirit realm. I look back over my life and I recall even before I was saved being sensitive to the hearts of others (sometimes to a fault). I have always had a love for what the world considers to be the *underdog*. This same truth followed me into Holiness…and still holds true today. As a true prophet, one knows how to put not only this flesh aside but also self and self-will for the sake of others. A true prophet will have a love and a longing to intercede for the people of God, what we refer to in the church as "standing in the gap." Whether it's the leaders or the backslider, the drug dealer who just gave his life to Christ or the prostitute getting high in the alley, it's the need to intercede; to reconcile that leads the true prophet. We have the ability to see past their mistakes, their calling, and even their past. We see more than just those things but we see their soul…and that's far more precious to God above all else.

'For as many as are led by the Spirit of God, they are the sons of God.' (Romans 8:14)

The differences between a true prophet and a false prophet are vast. I said it before and so I will say it again. There's a high price for the oil (anointing) that flows fresh from Heaven. You'll find a lot of folks who declare themselves prophets but not willing to pay the price for the oil. A prophet without the anointing is just a motivational speaker with talent. My question then is what yokes have you broken? Can you get a prayer through? Can you fast more than just a few hours for the people of God?

To be a true prophet God has to be able to trust you to walk circumspectly to the Word of God. You can't just live like anything and talk like everyone and call yourself a prophet. There must be a difference. The office of a prophet is a higher call to remain consecrated before God. Truth is God often requires you to be separated and by yourself. I look back over my life now and what I didn't understand then, I do now. To all those who walked away, for all the friends who thought all I do is go to church, and for the ones who left me out and we drifted apart, I understand. It was ordained of God.

This charge is a serious charge and I am honored that God would even consider me worthy. The weight of the glory is a heavy mantle. Not everybody is equipped to bear the weight. This life requires much prayer, much fasting, interceding, studying and being sensitive to the voice of God. Being a prophet you must be able to hear God speak over your own self, over your own emotions, over your will to sound important or your will to go off. It is important to speak truth into people's lives. I'm not talking about your version of the truth but REAL truth, God's truth.

> *'I will raise them up a Prophet from among their breth-*
> *eren, like unto thee, and will put my words in his*
> *mouth; and he shall speak unto them all that I shall*
> *command him.'* (Deuteronomy 18: 18)

In my early days when God would use me to prophesy to His people, of course I would always speak only as God instructed me to. Still, later I would often go home feeling like the prophet Jeremiah who often prophesied rebuke and correction to the children of Israel. I would later cry out to God in my prayer closet with tears flowing from my eyes. I wondered why He didn't allow me to speak supernatural blessings over the all saints; who seemed to me (that's in my flesh and my human reasoning) needed some *good news*.

> *'Howbeit when he, the Spirit of truth, is come, he will*
> *guide you into all truth: for he shall not speak of him-*
> *self; but whatsoever he shall hear, that shall he speak:*
> *and he will shew you things to come.'* (John 16:13)

Yet God revealed to me the words of a true prophet should edify the Body of Christ and turn the people's hearts' back to God. True prophesy births restoration, reform, renewal and true repentance to God's people. As the prophet speaks, the Spirit of God is conditioning the hearts and minds of the saints to receive the prophetic word. This we know that the Word of God is quick and alive. For by it we build upon the principles of Jesus Christ and not of ourselves.

First and foremost, I refuse to sit back and allow the enemy to come in my very presence and mock the power of God; false prophet, lying wonder, whatever s/he wishes to operate as. The devil is a lie! Stand with me, people of God, and fight against the kingdom of darkness. Fight for your families. Fight for your dreams. Fight for your destiny. Fight for what's right. Fight for the truth! God has given us the power to subdue kingdoms. We have the power to tear Satan's kingdom down and the lies he used to build it.

I speak now as a true prophet to those of you who lives line up with the Word of God and you who also have wrestled with the prophetic gift that the Spirit of God has imparted into you. Rise up prophet! Now is the time to walk in kingdom authority. Now is the time to fight the kingdom of darkness and all his lies like never before. Rise up! Embrace the divine call that is upon your life. Stop hiding behind your excuses and the spirit of fear. Speak out again sin! Be bold, be wise but speak and declare what the Spirit of the Lord is saying.

'Cry aloud, spare not, lift up thy voice like a trumpet, and shew my people their transgression, and the house of Jacob their sins.' (Isaiah 58:1)

I am Prophetess Natisha Wilson, a prophet to the nations. I am an ambassador of Jesus Christ. Therefore I am God's mouthpiece. I speak as God instructs me to speak. I declare the devil is a defeated foe! I stand in the authority of Christ of which I have been called by the power of the Living God, even Jesus Christ. Wake up people of God! By the power of God, I break the yokes of depression and deception that the enemy has used to manipulate and bound God's people. I abort every attack and assignment that the enemy designed to distract you from the purpose God has birthed in you. I bind every spirit of perversion, disobedience, rebelliousness and torment that has followed you this far. You are no longer bound! You are no longer captive to your past. Come out! I declare and decree you are free today! I come against every generational curse passed down in your family and the spirit of witchcraft and manipulation. I cancel every false prophet and every lie that was spoken over you. You will not be who your mother was. You are not your father's mistake. Your past is under the Blood of Jesus Christ. Let it go!   So what, you fell. Maybe they said you would never bounce back. That's a lie! Get up from there. Repent! Take up your bed and live again! Love again! Breathe! Be great! Be tenacious! You are who God called you to be! So be TRUE to YOU!

Chapter 10: *Moving Forward*

Unleashed! Unleashed! The prophecy is unleashed! My God! Let me just catch my breath for a second. Ah…I am here! I finally made it! After all I have gone through; I am free! God has brought me forward for such a time as this! You may not understand just what it took for me to make it here. Nevertheless, I AM HERE! It took me step-by-step and inch-by-inch with one foot in front of the other but God has divinely orchestrated my very footsteps. Talk about divine intervention. My God! I see it in the Spirit. I understand it all now. In order to move forward, I had to first be unleashed. Now let's move!

'Have not I commanded thee? Be strong and of a good courage; be not afraid, neither be thou dismayed: for the Lord thy God is with thee withersoever thou goest.' (Joshua 1:9)

Some of you, God had to rescue from domestic abuse with

black eyes and too much make-up. There were some of you who God had to rescue from the streets carrying a pocket full of dope surrounded by death and destruction. Even some of you, God had to save from sexual immorality selling your flesh just to make ends meet and looking for love in all the wrong places. Then there were some of you who God pulled from the very brinks of Hell when you were straddling the fence and playing church. So go ahead and be grateful for where God has brought you from. Can't nobody tell it like you can tell it. We ought to be thankful and bless Him continuously because of His grace and His mercy. Even still, today is a new day. It's time we move forward. Let's stop crying about it. Stop complaining about who walked away. Stop murmuring about what was. It's time out for blaming God for what could've been. Look past your THEN and see the NOW. God has prepared you for this move; for NOW is your time! Come out of the wilderness. God has unleashed you for NOW. So what are you waiting for? Move forward!

> *'The Lord God of your fathers make you a thousand times so many more as ye are, and bless you, as he hath promised you!'* (Deuteronomy 1:11)

By no means am I telling you something that I myself haven't had to go through as well. By the grace of God and despite the enemies' attacks…again, I AM HERE! I'll be remiss if I didn't say there were some days that I had to look in the mirror and speak to my own self. I had to speak to my own mind, my own heart and speak to my feet to move forward.

Listen, there are times when God will require you to move forward even when you don't know where God is moving you to. Look at Abraham. God required him to leave his father's house and go to a land he'd never seen or even dreamt of before. Yet he obeyed God and it was counted unto him as righteousness.

I can't speak for you, friend, but I have decided that after all that I've gone through including the good, the bad, and the ugly that I still must keep my perspective and be diligent in my pursuit in getting to my destiny. The moment I slow down or the moment I get distracted may be the very same moment that may cost me everything that I fought so hard for. Nor do I have time to cry over yesterday. Yesterday is dead and gone. I can't get back yesterday's tears. See, during this process I had to overcome disappointment, rejection, heartache, and fear and I would be delusional to look or even glance back now. Look at Lot's wife. It cost her, her life. I don't have time to slow down now! I am finally unleashed in the Spirit and I realized I wasted too much time. I am kicking doors open and I am bolting for my life!

Let me be clear. In order to obtain the peace of God, to get past all the baggage, or see the promises of God and get to your destiny, then you must first understand it's not just going to happen at the batting of an eye. It's not going to drop into your lap or come in a neat package with a bow waiting on your doorstep. No, you have to make it happen! It takes a concerted effort in moving forward. Maybe you didn't know then, but let me encourage you now; by the grace of God you can do it!

The real question is, are you desperate enough to keep

moving forward despite the circumstances that life brings? Sometimes we convince ourselves that we are desperate for change. Yet we begin to make every excuse why we lack the change needed in our lives. We allow doubt, procrastination, and fear of failure to creep into our minds. Where is your effort then? What hindered you from moving forward? We must push past these things. They are only stall tactics the enemy uses to stunt or halt our progress in God. Considering all the time that has past, God has finally brought you to this moment. Use it!

Man of God, Woman of God there is no last straw or last breath. This is not the hour to throw in the towel or to look at what was and what could have been. I declare and decree that you can't die here! Don't you dare faint. Don't you dare bend. You have the power to endure. God is calling you to cast off the spirit of heaviness and to put on the garment of praise. So go on and catch your breath. Inhale and exhale. Build with the momentum that God has birthed in you. You cannot afford to get stuck now with where you are. The time to move is NOW. Not tomorrow, not yesterday, but NOW! I then charge you to move NOW, Man of God. I then encourage you, Woman of God, to keep moving forward. God has unleashed in you the ability to prevail, to conquer, and to soar. God knows, you may never get this opportunity again.

> *'Being confident of this very thing, that he which hath begun a good work in you will perform it until the day of Jesus Christ...'* (Philippians 1:6)

If moving forward to you means moving from past relationships then stop reminiscing over old memories, past photos, and text messages. Just move! The same can be said if moving forward requires you to dream again. I know that the last time you attempted to build the business, push the ministry, branch out or fall in love didn't go as plan. However, trust me when I say that this time it's different. This time *you* are different. This time *I* am different. My anointing is different. Once God unleashed this prophetic call upon my life, I dream bigger. I fight, in the Spirit, fiercer. I trust God greater. Friend, you have the ability to succeed and claim all that God has given you dominion over. I challenge you to encourage yourself in the Lord. Praise God for even NOW! Man of God, you're still here! That's a blessing. Woman of God, you're still standing! It may have started out slow but God has enlarged your territory just as He said he would and He's laid it all at your feet. Now, seize it!

'God is not a man, that he should lie; neither the son of man, that he should repent: hath he said, and shall he not do it? Or hath he spoken, and shall he not make it good?' (Numbers 23:19)

See, moving is more crucial to the Body of Christ than actually just physically moving forward. It's more to it than just tracking steps and walking it out. It's all about trusting God. We trust Him no matter what; no matter who, no matter when, and no matter why. We understand this principle fact: *if I fail to move forward when God says move then I not only handicap my future but I abort my destiny.* (Now that's a Word)! My

God. My God.

'But as it is written, Eye hath not seen, nor ear heard, neither have entered into the heart of man, the things which God hath prepared for them that love him.' (1 Corinthians 2:9)

This season in your life will be unlike any other you've seen before it. God is changing the very course of history on your behalf. He's rewriting your story even now. For your faithfulness, God is changing all the rules and shifting all the key players. This season is the game changer. You will now see all the little pieces finally coming together. All the tears will finally began to make sense. The sacrifice wasn't for naught. The struggle was not in vain. Know that God can birth greatness even after extreme disaster. He specializes in what man calls the impossible. They may have expected you to fail. That was their mistake. They underestimated the God you serve. Man of God, Woman of God, the overflow is here and it's flooding your way. To get all that God has promised, you can't stop now. You've come too far. Keep moving forward!

'The Lord shall open unto thee his good treasure, the heaven to give the rain upon thy land in his season, and to bless all the work of thine hand: and thou shalt lend unto many nations, and thou shalt not borrow.' (Deuteronomy 28:12)

Here's a news flash. If you never go through then you'll

never come out. If you build a house on sand then I don't care how beautiful that house is, how many bedrooms it has or what neighborhood it's in that house will not stand. It will ultimately fail. So, it is with us. Christ is our Solid Rock! See, you can plan to go back to school for that master's degree, you can find the love of your life, you can record your first single, you can even leave your hometown and plant new roots across country just in your efforts to move forward. However, anytime you leave God out of the equation you're only moving in the opposite direction. The problem is without a solid foundation in Christ your next position becomes only a failed attempt and a false move. You are out of order!

You cannot move forward and be out of order or out of position with God. I don't care how much you try or what your agenda is. To move forward by any means, your life must line up with the Word of God. If you are out of order with God then everything you attempt to do is out of order. It will not work. Period.

Don't you see or don't you know the assignment upon your life is bigger than just you? We are in a war. We are engaged in battle. In this battle you must fight! Don't allow the enemy to catch you sleeping. Don't just apologize but repent! Don't just come to church but participate. You may not understand it but keep stepping in formation. The more the enemy wage war against me, the more I press in the Spirit. The more I press, the greater the attack. The greater the attack then the more I advance the Kingdom of God. I advance in my praise. I advance in the Word of God. I advance in the Spirit. I subdue kingdoms by the authority of which Christ has made me free. I

HAVE BEEN UNLEASHED! Man of God, Woman of God, whatever you have to do to move forward…you do it! If you need to get back in position then do it. If you need to get your house in order, then by God, just do it. God has given you the authority (the Holy Ghost) and the sword, which is the Word of God to rise up and march. Consider this your marching orders. March solider!

Like the prophet Ezekiel, I prophesy, as I am commanded, a fresh Word into your life. This prophetic anointing has been unleashed in me to tell you today that God is excelling you into new dimensions. Brace yourself for this prophetic shift! You are going to have to catch your breath for this next season because each blessing that is coming is going to come so sudden it's going to leave you breathless. The call upon your life is greater than you ever imagined. God said the anointing that's rest upon your life has already gone before you and spoken your name in great places so that when the door is open you would already be known before you get there.

Surely, as I am a Woman of God and carry this prophetic anointing as a true prophet, I prophesy that the mandate on your life is greater than every mistake, every failure, and every lie that you had to endure. You had to go through it so God could cause you to come forth and shine. Now is your time! You held on when everyone else let go. You endured the hardness even with tears in your eyes. You remained steadfast and unmovable despite the attacks of the enemy. God strengthened the warrior in you to stand. I can hear God saying, out of all the others, He placed in you this mantle to carry…to reach the lost, to restore the broken, to heal the sick, and subdue kingdoms.

You are a natural born innovator, a leader, and trailblazer in the Kingdom. God has unleashed YOU for such a time as this. God sent me to tell you don't just go after the dream, don't just write vison, and don't just speak the prophecy, but UNLEASH IT!

'The Lord shall command the blessing upon thee in thy storehouses, and in all that thou settest thine hand unto; and he shall bless thee in the land which the Lord thy God giveth thee.' (Deuteronomy 28:8)

- *THE END* -

About the Author

Prophetess Natisha E. Wilson is a dynamic, profound, anointed and consecrated Woman of God. She has purposed her life to the call of ministry as God's hands, feet and His mouthpiece. Prophetess Wilson serves faithfully in ministry at Lighthouse Apostolic Ministries Church of God in Saint Louis, Missouri on the advisory board as an ordained Evangelist, a Prophet, the Sunday School Superintendent, Vice President of Outreach and Mobile Ministry, and a vital part of the New Covert's for over 10 years.

Prophetess Wilson is a true vessel of honor set apart by God even from birth. At 16 years old she was born-again and filled with the Holy Ghost. She has been saved for 20 years now.

God allowed this fearsome prophetess to remain a virgin until she was married in 2006. She is married to Elder Jason R. Wilson, Sr., and has 3 beautiful children. They have been successfully married for 13 years.

Prophetess Natisha E. Wilson is specifically designed as a true prophet to the nations sent under the divine authority of God to be a key part of the Body of Christ for divine kingdom use and to win souls for Christ. She is a woman of prayer, purpose and perseverance. She is an End Time Prophet and an End Time Warrior in these last and evil days. God has brought her forward for such a time as this. Unable to restrain this gift any longer, she opens the door to her anointing and invites you to **Prophecy *Unleashed*.**

www.ingramcontent.com/pod-product-compliance
Lightning Source LLC
Chambersburg PA
CBHW031307060726
47590CB00003B/1091

- You will be requested to enter a passcode to secure your iPad. If you create **Touch ID**, you must use a passcode if in any case your fingerprint isn't acknowledged. Securing your computer data is an excellent idea, and the iPad provides you with several options. Tap password option to choose your lock method.

- You can arrange a Custom Alphanumeric Code (that is a security password that uses characters and figures), a Custom Numeric Code (digit mainly useful, however, you can add as many numbers as you want!) or a 4-Digit Numeric Code (a high old college pin!). In case you didn't install or setup **Touch ID** you may even have an option not to add Security password. Tap on your selected Security option.

- I would recommend establishing a 4-digit numeric

code, or Touch ID for security reasons but all optional setup is done likewise. Input your selected Security password using the keyboard.

- Verify your Security password by inputting it again. If the Password does not match, you'll be requested to repeat! If indeed they do match, you'll continue to another display automatically.

At this time of the set-up process, you'll be asked whether you have used an iPad before and probably upgrading it, you can restore all of your applications and information from an iCloud or iTunes backup by deciding on the best option. If this is your first iPad, you will have to get it started as new, yet, in case you are moving from Android to an iPad, you can transfer all your data by deciding and choosing the choice you want.

How to Restore iPad Back-up from iCloud or iTunes

If you want to restore your iPad from an iTunes back-up, you may want to connect to iCloud and have the latest version of iTunes installed on it. If you are ready to begin this process, tap **restore** from iTunes back-up on your iPad and connect it to your personal computer. Instructions about how to bring back your data can be followed on the laptop screen.

In case your old iPad was supported on iCloud, then follow the instructions below to restore your applications & data to your brand-new device:

- Tap *Restore* from iCloud back-up.

- Register with the **Apple ID** and Password that you applied to your old iPad. If you fail to recollect the

13

security password, there's a link that may help you reset it.

- The Terms & Conditions screen will show. Tap the links to learn about specific areas in details. When you are ready to proceed, select **Agree**.

- Your **iPad** will need some moments to create your **Apple ID** and hook up with the **iCloud server**.

- You will notice a summary of available backups to download. The most up-to-date backup will be observed at the very top, with almost every other reserve below it. If you want to restore from a desirable backup, tap the screen for ***all backups*** to see the available choices.

- Tap on the back-up you want to restore to start installing.

- A progress bar will be shown, providing you with

a demo of the advancement of the download. When the restore is completed, the device will restart.

- You would see a notification telling you that your iPad is updated effectively. Tap *Continue*.

- To complete the iCloud set up on your recently restored iPad, you should re-enter your iCloud (**Apple ID**) password. Enter/review it and then tap *Next*.

- You'll be prompted to upgrade the security information related to your *Apple ID*. Tap on any stage to replace your computer data, or even to bypass this option. If you aren't ready to do this, then tap *Next* button.

- **Apple pay** is Apple's secure payment system that stores encrypted credit or debit cards data on your device and making use of your iPad also with your fingerprint to make safe transaction online and with other apps. Select *Next* to continue.

- To ***feature/add a card***, place it on a set surface and place the iPad over it, so the card is put in the camera framework. The credit card info will be scanned automatically, and you will be requested to verify that the details on display correspond with your card. You'll also be asked to enter the *CVV* (safety code) from the personal strip behind the card. If you choose (or the camera cannot recognize your cards), you can enter credit card information by hand by tapping the hyperlink. You could bypass establishing **Apple Pay** by tapping ***create later***.

- Another screen discusses ***iCloud keychain***, which is Apple's secure approach to sharing your preserved security password and payment information throughout all your Apple devices. You might use *iCloud security code* to validate your brand-new device and import present data, or you might be asked to continue registering your keychain if it's your first Apple device. In case you don't want to share vital data with other devices, you should go to *avoid iCloud keychain* or *don't restore passwords*.

- If you selected to set up your **Apple keychain**, you'll be notified to either use Security password (the same one you'd set up on your iPad) or produce a different code. If you're making use of your iCloud security code, you should put it on your iPad when prompted.

- This will confirm your ID when signing on to an iCloud safety code; a confirmation code will be delivered via SMS. You may want to hyperlink your smartphone text code (if you have never distributed one with Apple already) so that the code may be provided as a text. Then enter this code to your iPad if requested, then select *Next.*

- You'll then be asked to create **Siri**. *Siri* is your own digital personal associate, which might search the internet, send communications, and check out data in your device and a lot more, all without having to flick via specific apps. Choose to create Siri by tapping the choice or start Siri later to skip this task for now.

- To set up and create **SIRI**, you will need to speak several phrases to the iPad to review your conversation patterns and identify your voice.

- Once you say every term, a tick will be observed, showing that it's been known and comprehended. Another phrase may indicate that you should read aloud.

- Once you've completed the five phrases, you will notice a display notifying that Siri has been set up correctly. Tap *Continue*.

- The iPad display alters the color balance to help make the screen show up naturally under distinctive light conditions. You can switch this off in the screen settings after the iPad has completed configuring it. Tap *continue* to continue with the setup.

- Has your iPad been restored? Tap begin to transfer your computer data to your brand-new iPad.

- You'll be prompted to ensure your brand-new iPad has enough power to avoid the device turning off in the process of downloading applications and information. Tap *OK* to verify this recommendation.

- You will notice a notification show up on your apps, to download in the background.

How to Move Data From Android

Apple has made it quite easy to move your data from a Google Android device to your new iPad. Proceed to the iOS app. I'll direct you about how to use the application to move your data!

- Using the iPad, if you are on the applications & data screen of the set-up wizard, tap *move data from Google android*.

- Go to the Play Store on your Google android device and download the app recommended by the set-up wizard. When it is installed, open up the app, select **Continue** and you'll be shown the *Terms & Conditions* to continue.

- On your Android device, tap *Next* to start linking your Devices. On your own iPad, select ***Continue***.

- Your iPad will show a 6-digit code which has to be received into the Google android device to set the two phone up.

- Your Google android device will screen all the data that'll be moved. By default, all options are ticked - so if there could be something you don't want to move, tap the related collection to deselect it. If you are prepared to continue, tap ***Next*** on your Google android device.

- As the change progresses, you will notice the iPad display screen changes, showing you the position of the info transfer and progress report.

- When the transfer is completed, you will notice a confirmation screen on each device. On your Android Device, select ***Done*** to shut the app. On your iPad, tap ***Continue Installing iPad***.

- An **Apple ID** allows you to download apps, supported by your iPad and synchronize data through multiple devices, which makes it an essential account you should have on your iPad! If you have been using an iPad previously, or use iTunes to download music to your laptop, then you should have already become an **Apple ID user**. Register with your username and passwords (when you have lost or forgotten your **Apple ID** or password you will see a link that may help you reset it). If you're not used to iPad, select doesn't have an Apple ID to create one for free.

- The Terms & Conditions for your iPad can be seen. Please go through them (tapping on more to study additional info), so when you are done, tap ***Agree***.

- You'll be asked about synchronizing your data

with iCloud. That's to ensure bookmarks, connections and other items of data are supported securely with your other iPad's data. Tap ***merge*** to permit this or ***don't merge*** if you'll have a choice to keep your details elsewhere asides iCloud.

- **Apple pay** is Apple's secure payment system that stores encrypted credit or debit cards data on your device and making use of your iPad also with your fingerprint to make safe transaction online and with other apps. Select *Next* to continue.

- To ***feature/add a card***, place it on a set surface and place the iPad over it, so the card is put in the camera framework. The credit card info will be scanned automatically, and you will be requested to verify that the details on display correspond with your card. You'll also be asked to enter the *CVV* (safety code) from the personal strip behind the card. If you choose (or the camera cannot recognize your cards), you can enter credit card information by hand by tapping the hyperlink. You could bypass establishing **Apple Pay** by tapping *create later*.

- Another screen discusses ***iCloud keychain***, which is Apple's secure approach to sharing your preserved security password and payment information throughout all your Apple devices. You might use *iCloud security code* to validate your brand-new device and import present data, or you might be asked to continue registering your keychain if it's your first Apple device. In case you don't want to share vital data with other devices, you should go to *avoid iCloud keychain* or *don't restore passwords*.

- If you selected to set up your Apple keychain,

you'll be notified to either use Security password (the same one you'd set up on your iPad) or produce a different code. If you're making use of your iCloud security code, you should put it on your iPad when prompted.

- This will confirm your ID when signing on to an iCloud safety code; a confirmation code will be delivered via SMS. You may want to hyperlink your smartphone text code (if you have never distributed one with Apple already) so that the code may be provided as a text. Then enter this code to your iPad if requested, then select *Next.*

- You'll then be asked to create **Siri**. *Siri* is your own digital personal associate, which might search the internet, send communications, and check out data in your device and a lot more, all without having to flick via specific apps. Choose to create

Siri by tapping the choice or start Siri later to skip this task for now.

- To set up and create SIRI, you will need to speak several phrases to the iPad to review your conversation patterns and identify your voice.

- Once you say every term, a tick will be observed, showing that it's been known and comprehended. Another phrase may indicate that you should read aloud.

- Once you've completed the five phrases, you will notice a display notifying that Siri has been set up correctly. Tap **Continue**.

- The iPad display alters the color balance to help make the screen show up naturally under distinctive light conditions. You can switch this off in the screen settings after the iPad has completed configuring it. Tap *continue* to continue with the setup.

- Has your iPad been restored? Tap begin to transfer your computer data to your brand-new iPad.

- You'll be prompted to ensure your brand-new iPad has enough power to avoid the device turning off in the process of downloading applications and information. Tap *OK* to verify this recommendation.

- You will notice a notification show up on your apps, to download in the background.

NB: Setting up as new iPad: Similar method, as described above, applies.

CHAPTER 2

Setting up Wi-Fi & Mobile Networks

Would you like to connect your iPad to the internet before you begin the utilization of several features, like email and the application store? Right here is a way for connecting your iPad to a guaranteed wireless network as well as your mobile data network for access to the internet.

You might have recently been linked to Wi-Fi through the preliminary iPad setup, however, if you didn't, or want to get on a particular wireless network, then this section of the manual is the correct one for you!

How to Connect Your iPad to Mobile Data

If you procure your iPad on a promo, you might in all probability have a month data bundle incorporated with the agreement. Allowing you to apply the internet if you are far-away from any Wi-Fi systems. This is set up automatically when you initially start your iPad, and that means you should manage to connect anywhere as long as there's a stable mobile network transmission strength! If this is not the situation, follow my brief steps below to discover the best way to get the mobile internet ready for use.

- From the home display, Tap on the configuration icon.

- In the predominant configurations listing, tap on Mobile data (depending on your network, you might see Cellular data as an alternative).

- Ensure the *Mobile data* is defined **ON** (green),

tapping the change to allow it if required.

- If this hasn't worked well, you might enter configurations manually for your unique network operator. To get into these configurations, scroll right down to Mobile data network and tap on it to gain access to an option generally called *APN*.

- You could additionally have the ability to re-download the configurations from your Sim card by scrolling to the low area of the APN configurations website and tap reset configurations.

- If none of the strategies gets you connected to a mobile data network, I would suggest contacting your mobile network issuer for additional help, as they are capacitated to sending the configurations without delay to your device from their end.

I'd suggest most effectively the utilization of Mobile internet for email messages and general web surfing. If you watch many movies or pay attention to many online pieces of music, you might use your computer data bundle very quickly and turn into getting billed extra sums in addition to your month-to-month invoice. Test with your network service provider to discover your computer data charge, and look at the telephone bill app to know your recent data for each month.

Connecting Your iPad to a Wi-Fi network

For connecting your iPad to a Wi-Fi network, you'll first need to find the security key for the network. This may be on the sticker at the back or source of your router, and it might be called a WEP Key, WPA Key, or Wi-Fi password. If you're uncertain, you could check up on the person that installs your network, or your web service provider.

When you have this data, you are equipped to start!

- From the home display screen, tap on the configuration's icon.

- Within the settings menu, select *Wi-Fi*.

- Make sure the WiFi switch is preparing to *ON* (green) if it's not from inception, tap the change to *enable/allow* it. Using the WiFi *ON*, your iPad will check out and screen all available systems. Choose your network's name from the list shown and tap on it.

- When prompted, enter the *Wi-Fi* security password. That is delicate, so be sure you don't mistype it, so when you are ready to continue, tap **Join**.

- When the iPad is installed to the network, you might visit a blue tick shown up on the network's name, and a radio image will be observed next to your mobile network's name at the very top level of the screen. Whenever your iPad is at the range of the network, and wireless is switched **ON**, it'll connect automatically.

Enabling and Disabling the iPad Internet Connection

How to Turn OFF your Wireless Connection

If your wireless connection is slow, you may want to turn it off for a short time to let you use mobile data as a substitute - be aware of lots of information you are probable to apply! Apple has made it very quick and smooth to do this.

Open Control Centre by swiping up from below the Display Screen. In Control Centre you will see a row of six spherical icons which might be White when the function is turned **ON** and Gray while it's **OFF**. The Wi-

Fi image must be the second icon from the left, so tap this to put it out.

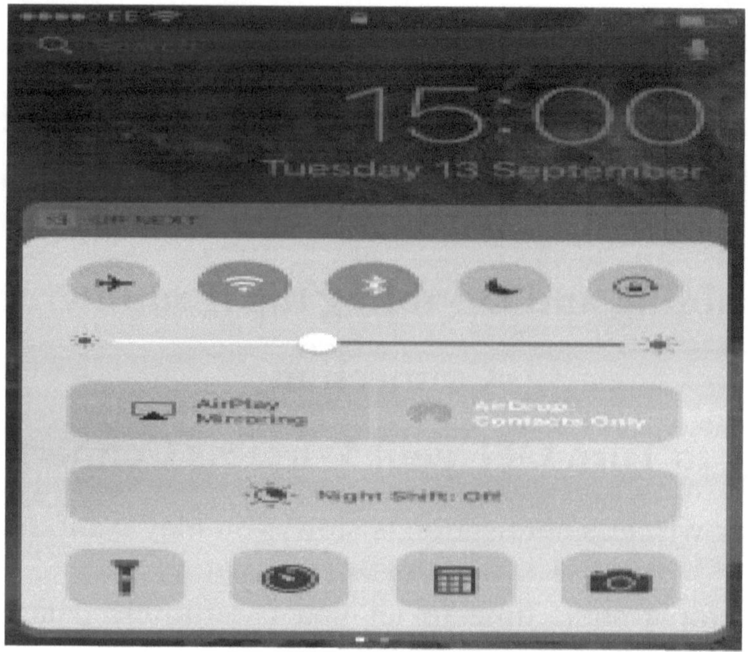

As soon as you have completed that, the wireless symbol next on your network name at the top of the display will disappear, displaying you're no longer linked to the internet. In case your iPad has a Sim card in it, the wireless image will be replaced by the data connection indicator (4G, 3G, E, GPRS) and you will be back again on Mobile Network. Just do not forget to turn your Wireless ON back to keep away from those pesky data charges!

How to Turn OFF Mobile Data

Your mobile data connection can be turned off in much the same way as Wi-Fi, but as it's not such a standard requirement, the setting to do so is buried a little deeper in the handset menus.

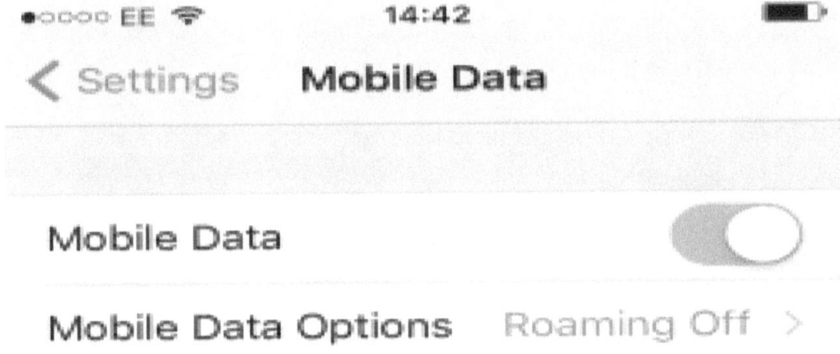

1.   From the Home screen, locate and tap on Settings.

2.   In the top section of the main settings menu, select

on Mobile or Cellular (you would see one word or the other, depending on your mobile network).

3.	At the top of the Mobile Data menu, there is a switch for Mobile Data. When enabled, the switch shows green. To turn off your data connection, tap the change. With your data connection turned off, your phone will only access the internet if you connect to a Wi-Fi network.

CHAPTER 3

How to Add & Import Contacts on Your iPad Tablets

When you have contacts on your old smartphone or device that you'll like to import to your brand-new iPad, please don't be worried I'll guide you!

Using Apple's iCloud service, you'll be able to import storage space documents and synchronize contacts simultaneously to your iPad.

If you have formerly been using an iPad, then transferring your contacts would be more comfortable by using ***Apple's iCloud Online Sync Service.***

In case your old mobile device has been installed to use iCloud, then your use of the same Apple identity (ID) on your iPad will deliver your contacts, calendar, and other information right to your brand-new device with no need for further action.

If you don't have iCloud installed on your old iPad, then it's the very first thing you will need to configure. Your old iPad should be associated with a Wi-Fi network so that people can reproduce or duplicate the info from your mobile phone to iCloud.

Do the following on your old iPad:

- Locate and tap the Configurations icon.

- Scroll down and select *iCloud*.

- If you see your address at the very top line, this means you're authorized directly into iCloud on your old iPad. If not, subscribe with the same Apple ID that you've used for your brand-new iPad.

- Turn internet network **ON.**

- Select the choice to Merge your computer data with **iCloud**. This will add all of your contacts to iCloud.

When you have already passed the initial set up the stage for your iPad, you might activate the iCloud services following precise instructions as stated above. When you're connected directly to iCloud, your contacts will start to download to your brand-new iPad immediately. If you have configured your old iPad to the iCloud service, all you have to do is select the option to use iCloud through the initial set up of your **iPad**, as well as your contacts that will automatically show up on these devices.

How to Import Contacts From a Blackberry Phone

To control your Blackberry contacts, we first need to transfer these to your computer. To do this, you must first download and set up the blackberry laptop software. As the software is installed, adhere to the instructions below!

- Connect your Blackberry to your laptop by using a micro USB cable for Blackberry processing device computer software to comprehend and identify the smartphone.

- Select Organizer at the left-hand panel of the program and tick the contacts field.

- While requested to choose the Sync Path, choose your laptop/computer only.

- Below contacts account, be sure home windows contacts is chosen. Press **OK** to continue.

- Press sync organizer at the right-hand part of the program to move your Blackberry contacts onto your home windows address book.

- Given that your contacts are saved in windows contacts, you can synchronize these details to your iPad through the iTunes software. If you have not already installed iTunes, download it from Apple's download website, making sure that your iPad isn't associated with your personal computer when you install the program.

- If iTunes is currently installed on your pc, connect your iPad through the provided USB cable and go through the Info Tabs near the top of the summary web page.

- Given that you're at the information tab, you will notice a tick box to Synchronize Your Contacts. Make sure that iTunes is defined to synchronize with your windows contacts; tick the package and press synchronize at the bottom left part of iTunes.

- Your contacts will now be shown on your iPad! If you have signed directly into iCloud on your mobile phone, your contacts will now start copying to Apple's cloud storage space service.

How to Import Contacts from a Windows Phone

To transfer contacts from a windows phone to your iPad, you'd first move the contacts to your home windows contacts program on your laptop. That is a reasonably reliable method, and also to learn more, keep reading!

- If you're migrating from a home windows phone and your mobile phone is linked to the internet, you ought to have Home windows Live (or

Hotmail) accounts already created on the smartphone. Under these events, your contacts can be stored on the Home windows live website by default. Go through the link and register with your home windows e-mail address and security password when prompted.

- Once you can see your contacts list, click a button near the top of the web page and choose Export from the dropdown list. Your contacts will begin installing as a .csv file on your personal computer.

- On your PC, go through the start menu and open up contacts.

- From the very best of the connection's windows, press import and choose CSV as your selected file type. Press import to save.

- Go through the search button to get the downloaded duplicate of your home windows live contacts. Once you've located it, press Next to start importing the contacts to your laptop's address folder.

- Given that your contacts are kept in windows contacts, you would be able to synchronize this data to your iPad through the iTunes program. If you haven't already downloaded iTunes from Apple's download web page, please do.

- If iTunes is currently established on your pc, connect your iPad via the provided USB cable and go through the *INFO* tabs near the top of the summary web page.

- Given that you're at the info tab, you will notice a tick-box to sync your contacts. Affirm that iTunes is defined to synchronize with your Home windows contacts, tick the field and press *SYNCHRONIZE* in the bottom left part of iTunes.

- Your contacts will now show up on your iPad! If you've signed on directly into iCloud on your mobile phone, your contacts will now start backing up just as much as Apple's cloud storage space service is enabled.

How to Import Contacts From A Google Android To iPad

Your Android device can export its contacts into a storage space file, the precise form of a written report which iCloud has is with the capacity of managing and absorbing. Once your links are in iCloud, it is only a matter of time expecting the info to complete synchronizing on your iPad. However, if you are uncertain how to actualize this stage, then examine the steps below to discover more!

If the contacts aren't on the Google account on your old

Android device, we'll need to get them there so that you can transfer these to your iPad, so that you will need to focus on step one as described below. If the contacts are already in your Google accounts, you may ignore this step.

To migrate your contacts out of your old Android device to your Google accounts:

- On your Android phone, tap the Contacts icon on your home display, or within the programs list.

- Tap the menu key, both as a button below the screen with three lines or the display screen button at the top-right corner, with three dots icon.

- Tap **Import/Export**. Several Android phones need you to press *More* before you start to see the *import/export settings*.

- Tap *Export to SDCARD*, or *Export to Storage Space* depending on your mobile phone.

- When exported and you're back viewing the contacts list, select the *menu key* again.

- Tap *Import/export,* as done in the third step.

- Tap import from **SDCARD** or *import from Storage space* depending on your mobile phone.

- If you are asked where to import the contacts to, tap Google or the Google E-mail address.

- Based on your specific phone, you'll be requested to choose which contacts to import. If so, pick all links. Your links will now be on your Google accounts!

Given that your contacts are on your Google accounts, you will extract these details and stick it onto the iCloud accounts such that it synchronizes to your iPad.

- On your laptop, head to Google's contacts website and subscribe with your Google email and password.

- From your Google contact, near the top of your contacts, press *More*, and consequently *Export*.

- Ensure that the all contacts radio field is ticked, in addition to memory cards format- Press *Export* to download your contacts on your computer.

- From your laptop's web browser, go to the iCloud website and register to make use of your Apple ID and Password.

- Go through the Contacts, a summary of all your contacts presently residing on your **iCloud account**.

- Press the configurations icon in the bottom-left part of the contacts page. This appears as though it's a cog or tool.

- From your menu which shows up, go through the import button, and navigate to your download folder. After picking your cards to import and Press Okay, your contacts will begin to show in iCloud! Within a few minutes, your iPad will start to show the same contacts too.

How to Add Contact to Your iPad Tablets Manually

We have discussed uploading your contacts from your previous device; however, when you begin using your device, you will want to add contacts as you go and edit or update the info of individuals you already have. Don't worry; you will become familiar with that now.

How to Add a New Contact

To include a completely new contact on your iPad, follow the instructions described below:

- Tap on the Contact App on your home Display.

- You might see any previously existing contacts on your display. To include a brand-new contact, select the blue+ at the very top right-hand nook.

- Enter the name of your brand-new contact in the areas supplied near the top of the screen. To add a mobile number, tap **add mobile**. Tap where it says Telephone to input the number, and you'll change the label home to a choice of yours by tapping it and selecting your desired from a list. To include an electronic email address, tap add E-mail, so that as you scroll down, you might see areas for additional input information, comprising home address, birthday, or even established custom ringtones and message shades for the contact.

- If you are satisfied with the info you have in your brand-new contact, tap *completed* at the very top right-hand nook to save the contact.

- Tap All Contacts at the very top left-hand nook to go again to your contact list.

Once you have stored your contact, select + to feature or add every other or tap the home button to come back to your home screen.

How to Edit iPad Contact

Editing a contact on your iPad isn't expected to vary from including a new one, just can be seen barely in yet another way.

To edit a contact:

- Open up the Contacts application from the home

display.

- Please scroll down and select the contact you want to edit, to open up it.

- At the very top right-hand corner, tap *Edit*.

- Now you can edit the contact's details as explained above, adding or changing the info as required. If you want to delete any data from a contact, select the pink group icon left of the sphere and tap delete at the right of the range.

- If you wish to delete the contact completely, scroll downwards and select *delete the contact*.

CHAPTER 4

How to Secure iPad with Lock Screen

On an iPad, you have a preference among a Custom Alphanumeric Code (that is a password with the use of letters and numbers), a Custom Numeric Code (figures only, however as many digits as you prefer!) or a 4-Digit Numeric Code (a fantastic old style pin!). You will need to decide which you need to use, so it is worth considering that earlier than you dive into the settings.

- Tap on the configuration icon, then scroll down and Tap on ***Touch ID & Password***.

- In the **Touch ID** & Password menu, tap the blue hyperlink to turn Password ON.

- The default Security password placing is a Custom Alphanumeric Code - a complex password containing letters and digits. You could alternate this by tapping Password options.

- Tap your chosen password option to select it.

- Enter your **PASSWORD**. While you type in your secret four-digit, the display screen will increase automatically.

- Re-input your Security password to verify it. If the entered Passwords do not match, you might be returned to the first Security password access display to start over. If the Password that has been entered matches, then you will go back to the Security password menu.

- The final element to decide is how fast you want to enter your Password, which is often a balance between usability and safety. To change this setting, Tap **Require Password**.

- Pick your time out from the listing on screen by

tapping the interval you want to set. A tick will appear on that line, and when you're happy with the setting, tap Back at the very top left-hand nook.

You can allow access to certain functions of your iPad when the screen is locked. There are switches to enable the usage of *NOTIFICATIONS, SIRI*, and other components of the working gadget. Tap any of these to permit them (when **ON**, the switches can look green).

How to Set Up Touch ID to Unlock Your iPad

Now that you have set up a Password, you may want to enable **Touch ID**, which is fingerprint recognition to unlock your Devices (meaning you might not need to type in that password, even though you could if you want to!).

Follow the instructions below to achieve this effortlessly;

- To begin setting up **Touch ID**, you will want to be within the Settings **Menu**.

- In the predominant settings menu, select **Touch ID & Password.**

- Input your **Password** to access the settings.

- Tap **Add a Fingerprint**.

- To start including your fingerprint, place your finger or thumb onto the ***Home button***, however, do not press it. Lift and replace your finger as instructed on-screen, shifting it very slightly as you achieve this. When the center of your fingerprint has been scanned, you'll be requested to place your finger in unique positions on the home button to experiment the edges.

- While your fingerprint is fully scanned, you will

see the whole screen, displaying that your print has been captured and Touch ID is ready. Touch **Continue**.

- As you add fingerprints, they'll be numbered. You can change the names (so you recognize which print is which) or delete fingerprints from the phone by Tapping the name after which editing or deleting as required.

- When you've modified the name of fingerprint, Tap **Done** on the keyboard to keep the new name.

- **TOUCH ID** will be without delay activated for unlocking your iPad, and for **Apple Pay**. To enable iTunes and App Store Purchases to be authorized alongside with your fingerprint, Tap the switch to carefully turn it **ON,** then get into your Apple ID password.

You can upload as much as five Fingerprints, so putting

in place fingerprint access for your family members may be carried out too. A phrase of warning though; remember that in case you've introduced the capacity to use fingerprint scanning to authorize iTunes and App Store buys, anybody who's fingerprint is added can do this too!

CHAPTER 5

How To Add Email Account(s)

The iPad allows multiple POP3, IMAP, and other accounts. If you have one email, take into account one for work and another one for private/home, getting all of your emails is as simple as adding every of the account on your iPad.

- To commence, select the *Configurations icon.*

- In the configurations, find and tap on Email, on another page, tap on Account to add.

- At the right-hand side, tap ***ADD ACCOUNT***.

- Choose your E-mail providers (e.g. Google, Yahoo, Live, etc…) from the list shown. Mail Accounts is often utilized by companies and network service providers, live.com is the new name for a Hotmail or windows live accounts, and YAHOO!,

GOOGLE and AOL are self-explanatory. For another e-mail company, select *OTHER* followed by tapping ***ADD Email Account***.

- Review your **EMAIL** and Security password (aside from some other data required, alongside your name) as asked, and Tap **Next** or **Register** on the screen to continue.

- If the account(s) is established, you may review your details was successfully founded, or a data screen about how exactly your e-mail accounts can be utilized. You might allow this or tap **Next** to continue.

- This may then automatically spread to show notifications to be able to pick and choose which data the accounts will use on your new iPad - email, connections, calendars, and probably different items too, with regards to the accounts.

Turn OFF notifications for just about any items you do not need to be on your iPad, then select **Save**.

- Once completed, you should see your accounts in the list at the right-hand part of the screen.

In case your e-mail account does not install or get created, you'll be requested for additional information regarding the account, which includes incoming email server settings. You might contact them simultaneously for help. Once you've introduced your accounts, you could gain access to your email messages by tapping the email icon on your home screen. When you have installed several electronic mail accounts, you might view all your emails in a single inbox by selecting the ***ALL INBOXES*** option from the mailbox section in the e-mail app.

CHAPTER 6

Sending Emails & Attachments from iPad

To send an email, you ought to have already created an email account on your iPad.

- Find and open the app on your home display screen. This looks like a White Envelope, and if you've acquired emails already, there may be a pink badge on it which represents some unread email messages.

- The email App will open up your brand-new E-mail. To view your inbox, Tap **INBOX or ALL INBOXES** at the top left-hand nook of the screen.

- When you can see your E-mail inbox, select the **COMPOSE BUTTON**. This looks like a pen and paper, and it's located at the top-right nook of the email inbox screen.

- The screen will now show blank email, ready to begin writing.

- New emails will regularly send from your default electronic mail account (which is usually the first one you have added). When you have multiple accounts on your iPad and want to switch the accounts to send from, it is easy to do. Touch the **CC/BCC, FROM** collection which shows the e-mail address with which you're sending from, then Touch the e-mail address shown to change it to another account.

- To add a **recipient**, Tap into the **TO** field. To browse your contact list, Tap the + button at the right-hand aspect of the display. You could additionally start to type their name, and any matching contacts would be shown allowing you to pick the one you are searching out for. In case you don't have the Tap saved for your device already, simply Tap the **TO** Field and start typing the E-mail address you wish to send to.

- Utilize the **SUBJECT** box to add a title to your e-mail.

- Tap into the main window (above the pre-loaded send from my iPad signature) to put the cursor there and type your message. When you're ready to send your e-mail, select **Send** at the top right-hand nook.

How to Add an Attachment to E-Mail

iPads can feature photos and videos from the device as an attachment ever since iOS 7 was launched in 2013. However, you can now additionally add attachments from online storage including Google Drive or Dropbox, especially with the recent **iOS 13, iOS 12 and iOS versions** to come.

How to Attach an Image or Video From Your iPad

- Begin by creating and accessing your email account as stated above.

- To feature/attach a picture or video, Tap the **CAMERA** icon to the right of the keyboard's top level.

- Please navigate through the image folders you've created for your iPad to discover the image or video you want to transfer and Tap it to choose it.

- To choose the image or video and connect it for your email, Tap **USE**. You can attach one at a time. However, nothing is stopping you from adding any other one!

- Provided that you've launched your internet connection, Tap **SEND** to get it sent immediately.

How to Add a Document From an Online Storage App

To add accessories from a web storage account such as **Dropbox or Google Drive**, you'll need to have the App for that service installed on your iPad and be signed directly into your account in the App to gain access to your documents.

- Create your email as described above, then select the paper clip icon to the right of the keyboard's top line.

- By default, your **iCloud Drive Storage** will open. If that is where your file is, navigate through your folders and choose it. To import an item from external storage, Tap **SOURCE**.

- The first time you use this feature, you'll want to allow access to which you will use an option storage space source. Tap **More**.

- The manage location display allows you to select the storage Apps you want to include documents from elsewhere. Tap the switch to the right of your preferred App to allow/enable it (it turns green) then Tap **DONE**.

- You'll then be back at the **iCloud Drive Screen**. Tap Source once more to open up your storage choices.

- This time all the storage space Apps you enabled in the previous display screen should be accessible for you in the menu. Tap the Appropriate one to discover the files and folders therein.

- Please navigate through the folders to locate the file you are considering, and Tap it to attach it to your email.

- When you've attached your document(s), Tap **SEND** to get document attached and sent to your contact(s)!

CHAPTER 7

How To Proceed Whenever Your iPad Email Does not Work

Among the predominant benefits of the iPad is it will keep you connected to almost anybody from anywhere. Whether it's by text, social press, or e-mail, your iPad is your marketing communications lifeline to the world. That is one of the things that makes it so irritating whenever your e-mail is no longer working (it's so annoying if you would like to get an electronic email for your business or job).

You'll find so many issues that could affect your iPad form downloading e-mail, which explains why this section is entirely for you if you're confronted with email challenges.

You will find eight predominant steps you might use to try and solve the majority of the challenges you might be facing with e-mail.

We shall start highlighting them individually.

- **Check Your Network Connection**

Your iPad cannot get an e-mail if it's not linked to the internet. It's essential to get access to a mobile network through your phone or a Wi-Fi network that may grant you access to e-mail.

You need to additionally ensure that Airplane mode is not enabled on your iPad because that could quickly block contacts to mobile and Wi-Fi networks.

- **Restart Your Email App**

One quick way to repair any application not operating as

anticipated is to exit and re-launch the application. That is another simple method of solving mail difficulties. To try out this method, follow the next steps:

1.   Double select your iPad Home button.

2.   When the multi-tasking view shows up, find Mail.

3.   Swipe Email up and close the display.

4.   Click once on the Home button.

5.   Tap the Mail application to re-launch it.

- **Restart Your iPad**

If regardless your web connection is intact and you've restarted the email app, and you also see that the problem persists, the next step is one of the most typical in every **iPad-troubleshooting guide** which is to restart your smartphone.

Sometimes it's hard for individuals to trust because we

always expect that organic approach must be employed to solving problems; however, in most instances, a simple method usually is our best bet. So; restarting an iPad can get rid of loads of issues. Sometimes your mobile phone needs a new start-up.

- **Upgrade Your iPad iOS version**

Among the top method of troubleshooting is to ensure you have the latest version of the iOS working on your device. An updated version of the iOS fixes bugs in today's version on your phone automatically and update its functions. Practically, the problems with your e-mail is a harmful bug program which can best be set with the latest iOS upgrade or your e-mail provider has made a few changes to their configurations, and it's only the latest iOS version to guide you to cope with the change.

- **Delete, and Set-up E-mail Accounts Again**

If none of the steps enumerated above solved the issue, there might not be anything wrong with your iPad. On the other hand, the problem can also be from the configurations used to try reference to your Email accounts. Perhaps; if you enter a wrong server address, username, or security password when establishing the accounts on your iPad, you might not be capable of getting an Email.

If this is the case, you can begin once more by deleting the e-mail accounts from your mobile phone following a few steps below:

1.   Head to Settings.

2.   Go directly to the Tabs where you see Email, Contacts, and Calendar.

3.   Go through the accounts with the problem.

4.   Delete the Accounts.

5.	Delete from My iPad in the pop-up menu in the bottom of the screen.

Having deleted the e-mail accounts, check all the settings that you can use to gain access to this accounts and feel the procedure of adding an e-mail account in your iPad again (you might synchronize the reports to your phone through iTunes).

There are many other ways of deleting an email account from an iPad; this and many other important information would be explained explicitly in a later edition of this book.

- **Contact Email Provider**

As of this juncture, it's time to get some excellent direct technical support for your e-mail issues.

An excellent approach is to check with your e-mail provider, such as (Google for Gmail, Yahoo, and many more.). Each Email service provider has specific ways to provide support; however, a great strategy is to log into your email accounts on the internet through a pc and then navigate to your company support link.

- **Make an Apple Store Appointment**

In case your email provider can't help, you might have a problem that is complex than you are designed for. If so, it is the best shot that you should take your iPad-and all the info about the e-mail account-to the nearest Apple Store for tech support team (you could additionally call Apple for support). Apple stores are usually occupied, so be sure to make a scheduled appointment before moving out to avoid waiting around all day long at their offices.

- **Check Your IT Department**

If regardless you're trying to check a work Email

accounts, and if the first five steps didn't work, it is most possible that the problem doesn't tally with your iPad whatsoever. The problem may be from the email server you want to download email from. When there is a brief concern with that server or a construction change that you aren't aware, that could impact and stop your iPad from being able to access it. So if the e-mail account is from your workplace, I'll recommend you contact and talk with the IT division for a solution.

CHAPTER 8

How To Use App Store To Find Applications

Do you want to download apps to your iPad? With such a lot to choose from in the app store, it's hard to realize where to begin! Right here's the way to get the tasty morsels of application from the Apple application store for your iPad.

How to Download New App on iPad

Downloading new applications via the app store is a reasonably direct process; however, when you download your first app, you can have a bit of set up to do in regards to your **Apple ID**. Comply with the instructions underneath, and you will have your iPad ever downloading apps right away!

- To begin, tap the App Store icon at the home screen of your new iPad.

- The store will open up with the Featured Apps web page. This may display to you the applications presently being promoted, either by Apple themselves or via the App developers. You can scroll down the page to look at distinct sections, and each areas' icons can be swiped through to examine which apps are being featured.

- Tapping **See All** at the right-hand side of every featured segment will show you that option in more detail.

- At the top left of the first website, you could select on **Categories**, which breaks up the App Store into broadly titled segments, without difficulty navigating through the sections. Tap **Cancel** at the top to return to the presented apps web page.

- In the categories, you may see sub-categories to make it simpler to browse the kind of apps you're looking for.

- At the bottom of the leading web page, you'll find links to various sections of the App Store. Featured you will see, and top Charts which are self-explanatory - brief access to **"Top 40 applications"** style lists of free and paid applications if you want to scroll through.

Explore allows you to look for what human nearby are downloading, which can be quite useful when trying to find your way around a new location, or in case you're at a sporting or musical occasion.

Tapping **SEARCH** at the lower part of the display screen allows you to enter the name of an App you have heard about or recommended to you.

Updates, as the name implies, is where you can control your apps and download updates.

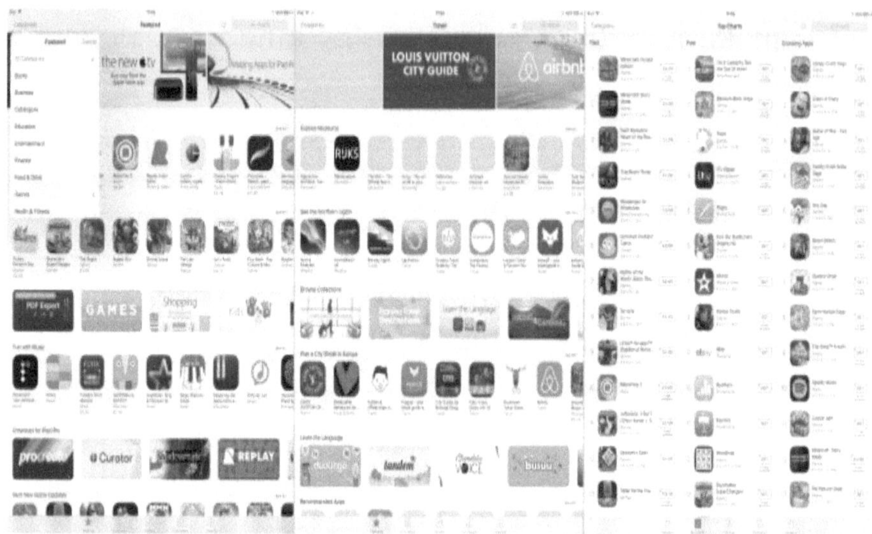

- When using the search function, anything you type into the field causes results to auto-fill on the web page. Tap the Search suggestion you like, to see what apps it brings up.

- If the button to the right-hand side of the app's name says **Download**, the app is free, and there will be no price to yourself. Tapping the word

Download will change the box to say **Install**.

- Tapping Install will start the download process. If there is a fee, the price would be displayed in place of the term **Download**, and you'll be asked to link a card to your **Apple ID** to pay for this and any future purchases.

- If that is the first app you have attempted to download on your new iPad, you may be requested to input your **Apple ID** information. If you have already got an **Apple ID** (if this is your first iPad you will be prompted to create one at some stage in the initial set up process), you can tap use existing **Apple ID**, and **Sign in**. In case you do not have an Apple ID, select create a new Apple ID and observe the on-screen instructions to create your free Apple ID account. When you have already introduced your Apple ID by signing into iCloud, you will need to put in your password.

- For ease of use, you may set a time hold of 15 or more minutes before your password is needed again. This can make it smooth to install several apps in one session as you may not need to enter your password every time. Tap to regularly require your security password or require after 15 minutes, as you deem fit to you.

- You'll necessarily need to accept the iTunes Terms & Conditions, and the Apple privacy policy (which you can get dispatched to yourself via email by tapping the supplied hyperlink) by tapping **Agree**, then show that you genuinely do agree by tapping **Agree** again!

- With your account signed in and the agreements handled, your app can now be downloaded. Tap ok for this to happen.

- When the application is downloading, you'll see a blue development indicator in the shape of a circle, with a square at the middle. Tap this if you want to pause/restart the download for any cause.

- When the application has been successfully installed, the progress button changes to an open button to which will let you access the app. When installing, the app will also appear in the first available home display area. However, you can without difficulty move this in case you want!

While you've completed your task in the store, press the **Home button** at the bottom of the iPad's front panel to return to your home display screen. Swipe across to see your newly installed apps!

How to Manage Apps on iPad
How to re-arrange iPad Apps

Whenever you download a brand-new app, it is automatically going to primarily occupy the next available space on your home display. You can easily re-arrange the applications into any order you want. To try this, tap and hold your finger on the application icon for some seconds. All the icons start jiggling. Now, all you want to do is place your finger on the image you need to move and drag it to the precise position of your choice. You can walk in between the display screen by moving the icon at the edge of the screen for a 2nd or 3rd. When you have finished, press the home button to go back to the standard display.

How to Organize iPad Folders

Setting your apps in folders makes it loads quickly to search out the app you're searching. In preference to scrolling through pages of apps, you could click on the appropriate folder and go immediately to the app you want.

To create a folder, all you need to do is place your finger on an app icon until it starts to jiggle similarly to when you are re-arranging apps. Then pull and drop an application icon at the top of another app icon. This will place both applications in a folder. You may change the name of the folder and move in a few more apps if you need. If you have completed the process, press the home button.

To move objects out of a folder, open up the folder first then maintain your finger on one of the application icons in it until they jiggle, then tap and hold on your selected

app, and drag it out of the folder to the home screen. If

you pull the remaining last app out of the folder, the

folder itself will vanish.

How to Delete iPad Apps

When you have downloaded an application which you do

not like or that you don't need again, you may delete it

off your iPad. To do that, just press and keep your finger

on the app icon till the icons begin jiggling about. You

ought to then see an **X** at the top left corner of every icon.

Tap the **"x"** to dispose of the app. Do not worry; you

cannot take away inbuilt apps on phone or contacts by

doing this so that it won't cause any problem.

CHAPTER 9

How to Proceed When You Can't Activate Used iPad

If you buy a used iPad, it is interesting. In the end, you come with an iPad and stretch your budget by acquiring a used one, especially for individuals who are not economically buoyant.

Some individuals encounter this issue along the way of activating their new device: The iPad will inquire further for somebody else's Apple ID and wouldn't typically work unless supplied.

This isn't a challenge that can't be fixed, so do not fret because you'll get it fixed following these steps.

- It is consequently an attribute of Apple's Find my iPad service known as activation lock.

- Activation Lock is a security measure that Apple

raised to cope with the allergy of iPad thefts. In earlier years, if someone takes an iPad without blockage by lock feature, they could clean it, resell it, and breakout with the crime. Activation lock altered the situation.

- When the initial owner setup finds my iPad on the tool, the **Apple ID** used will be stored on Apple's activation servers together with almost every other information about the phone. The activation servers will most effectively unlock the phone again if that unique Apple ID can be used. If you no more have the Apple ID, you'll never be in a position to activate or use the tablet. This facilitates the security of your iPad because nobody would like to grab a tablet they can't use. On the other hand, it generally does not harm you if you recently procure the phone.

- Dealing with activation lock is annoying, but additionally, it is smooth to solve. It's mainly possible, and the prior consumer just forgot to carefully turn off find my iPad or erase the tool correctly before offering it on the market (though it could also be a sign you've purchased a stolen device, so be cautious).

- You should contact the preceding owner of the telephone for him/her to consider the necessary steps.

How to Remove Activation Lock on iPad

- It is expedient that you should unlock or remove activation lock from the acquired iPad (used iPad) by inputting the prior owners' **Apple ID.** This technique can be initiated by getting in contact with the owner and detailing the scenario.

- If the owner lives near to you, I'll recommend that you hand over the phone back to him/her with the mission to insert the mandatory unlock code which is his/her Apple ID. When the seller gets the iPad at hand, he/she only will enter the necessary Apple ID on the activation lock display. Having done such, restart the telephone and then forge forward with the typical activation process.

Ways to Remove Activation Lock using iCloud

Sometimes, things can get a bit messy and complicated if the merchant/seller cannot physically access the tablet thanks to circumstances such as distance among other factors. This may also be resolved effortlessly as the owner may use iCloud to eliminate the activation lock from the phone through his accounts by following the steps below:

- Visit iCloud.com on any device, either mobile or laptop.

- Log-on with the Apple ID he/she used to activate the telephone.

- Click Find My iPad.

- Select All Devices.

- Go through the iPad you sold or want to market.

- **Select Remove from Accounts.**

Having achieved that, after that, you can PULL THE PLUG ON the iPad, and you switch it ON again. After that, you can proceed with the standard activation process.

How to Fix Locked Home-Screen or Security

Password

If you activate your phone and find out either the iPad's home display screen or the security password lock display, therefore that the supplier/vendor didn't completely erase the smartphone before offering it for you. On this notice, you'll need the owner to wipe these devices to be able to do it with the activation process.

The next two procedures should be followed as you hand over the phone to the owner or seller to unlock the phone;

- If the tablet works on iOS 10 and later version, the owner has to log out of iCloud and subsequently erase these devices by heading *to Settings -> General -> reset -> Erase All Content* and *Settings.*

- If the tablet works on iOS 9, the seller/seller must go to *Settings -> General -> reset -> Erase All*

Content and *Settings* and enter his/her Apple ID when prompted.

- When the erase process is completed, you're absolving to activate your phone with no further ado or hold off.

How to Wipe an iPad Using iCloud

Imagine if you can't gain access to the vendor/merchant due to some reasons, yet you will need your mobile phone to be wiped entirely for easy convenience, the seller may use iCloud to erase it. This is attained by ensuring the phone you want to get triggered linked to a WiFi network or mobile data network, and then inform the seller to follow along with the next steps:

- Visit http://iCloud.com/#find

- Sign in with the Apple id he/she applied to the

phone that is with you or sold to you.

- Click *All Devices*.

- Choose the phone sold you or available to you.

- Select *Erase iPad*.

- When the phone is erased, click *Remove from Accounts*.

- Restart the phone, and you are all set.

How to Erase an iPad Using Find My iPad App

This process is very much indeed identical to the approach explained above using iCloud by just using the Find my iPad application installed on some other iPad device. If the owner prefers to get this done, connect the phone you're buying to Wi-Fi or mobile data, and then inform the owner to adhere to the steps below:

- Start the *find my iPad* app.

- Sign on with the Apple ID they applied to the phone sold
  to you.

- Choose the phone.

- Tap *Actions*.

- Tap *Erase iPad*.

- Tap *Erase iPad* (It is the same button, however on a new
  display).

- Enter *Apple ID*.

- Tap *Erase*.

- Tap *Remove from Accounts*.

  - Restart the iPad and get started doing the setup
    process.

CHAPTER 10

How to Connect iPad to your TV Wirelessly and Cable

The iPad remains a great way to take pleasure in movies and TV, specifically when viewing on that beautiful 12.9-inch iPad Pro. This makes the iPad an unusual way to slice the wire and get rid of cable. Moreover, the newest TV app requires this step further, adding a centralized spot to control all of your loading apps. For everyone who've hunted through each application looking for which channels a specific film or show, we thank Apple!

However, how about watching your TV? If you'd opt for viewing on your large screen, don't get worried, it is on the other hand easy to get your iPad linked to your Television. You can also get it done wirelessly! Plus, you can connect your headphones to any Television to get a non-public watching experience.

Connecting the iPad to your TV with Apple TV and Airplay

Apple TV is an excellent way of connecting your iPad to your Television. While it is expensive over other alternatives, it's the most reliable solution that is mobile. This implies you will keep your iPad on your lap and utilize it as a remote control while sending the screen to your Television. This is the best and quality solution for video games, where using a cord to hook up your iPad on your Television may be prescribing or restricting.

Apple TV uses Airplay to have a connection/interaction with your iPad. Most loading apps use airplay and send full-display screen 1080p video to it. However, even applications that don't support Airplay or video out will continue to work via screen mirroring, which replicates your iPad's screen on your Television.

Various other bonus of Apple TV is the applications already installed on these devices. If you love *Netflix, Hulu plus* and *crackle*, you certainly do not need to add your iPad to see loading video from these services. The applications run natively on Apple TV. **Apple TV** additionally works amazingly with the iPad and iPod, letting you stream video through Airplay or use your entertainment device's audio speakers to try out music.

Apple currently arrived with a fresh release of Apple TV that works at the same processor used for the iPad air. This helps it be lightning swift. It additionally helps a complete-blown version of the application store, which provides usage of even extra apps. Regrettably, the access-level charge is $149 as at the time of research. The freshest information is the classic (old) Apple TV still works just superb, allowing you to connect your iPad on your TV's display and is currently designed for around $69 as at the time of research.

Connecting the iPad Wirelessly without the utilization of Apple TV via Chromecast

In case you don't have to head the Apple TV path; however nevertheless need for connecting your iPad to your TV without any wires, **Google's Chromecast** can be an alternative solution. It comes with an extraordinarily easy setup process that uses your iPad to configure the Chromecast and get it connected to your Wi-Fi network, and when the whole lot is established and operating, you might connect the iPad's screen to your television - as long as the application you are using, works with Chromecast.

Also, that's the best restricting factor when compared with Apple TV: Chromecast support wants to be included in the app when compared with Apple television's Airplay, which fits with almost every application for the iPad.

Why use *Chromecast*? For just one factor, it's much less costly. You could buy a Chromecast for as cheap as $30. It will work with both Google android and iOS devices; if you come with an android phone with your iPad, you might use chromecast with all of them. Moreover, with android, chromecast has a function much like Apple TV's screen mirroring.

Connecting the iPad to your High Definition TV through HDMI Cable

Apple's digital AV adapter is most likely the very best & most straight-ahead way to hook your iPad up to your High definition TV. This adapter lets you connect an HDMI cable from your iPad to your Television. This wire will send the video out to your Television. This means any application that helps video out will arrive in 1080p "HD" quality.

Moreover, preferably Apple TV, the digital AV adapter works with show mirroring, so even applications that do not support video away will screen up to your Television set.

Are you concerned about battery life?

The adapter additionally gives you access for connecting

a USB cable to your iPad that can source power to the unit and keep maintaining that battery from running low when you are binging on Seinfeld or doing other things. You could additionally stream your film collection from your laptop to your iPad via your High definition TV using home posting. This is a long notch process to finally change from DVD and Blu-ray to digital video without dropping the "to view it" on your substantial display TV. You can purchase the apple lightning digital AV adapter on amazon.

Consider: The lightning connector cannot work with the first iPad, iPad 2 or iPad 3. You may want to buy a digital AV adapter with a 30-pin connection for those old iPad models. This makes an Airplay solution like Apple Television even far better for these models.

Connecting an iPad through Composite/Component Cables

In case your TV does not support HDMI, or if you're genuinely working low on HDMI outputs on your HDTV, you can also choose to connect the iPad for your TV with composite or component cables. The amalgamated adapters break up the video to red, blue and green that provides a somewhat better picture, but amalgamated adapters are best designed for the old 30-pin adapters. Component adapters use the one 'yellowish' video wire well suited with the red and white audio cables, that's appropriate for almost all television sets.

The component and composite cables won't support the display mirroring mode on the iPad, so they could only use applications like Netflix and YouTube that support video out. Additionally, they flunk of 720p video;

therefore, the high-quality will never be as the digital AV adapter or Apple Television.

Unfortunately, these accessories might not be accessible to the more recent lightning connector, so; you'll need a lightning to 30-pin adapter.

Connecting the iPad with a VGA Adapter

Using Apple's VGA adapter, you could hook your iPad up to television outfitted with a VGA input, a pc monitor, a projector, and other display devices that supports VGA. That is amazing for screens. Many modern video screen units aid several display properties; you might even switch between your use of your display screen for your processing device and utilizing it for your iPad.

The VGA adapter will also support the screen mirroring mode. However, it generally does not transfer sound, and that means you will either pay attention through the iPad's built-in sound system or exterior speakers founded via the iPad's headphone jack.

If you're making programs on viewing through your TV, the HDMI adapter or the component cables will be the best solutions. However, if you intend on utilizing a laptop screen or want to use your iPad for big shows with a projector, the VGA adapter could be an excellent solution.

Do you realize you can view live Television on your iPad? There are many add-ons made to help you watch live Television on your iPad, access your cable stations and even your DVR from any room inside and while abroad through your computer data connect.

CHAPTER 11

How Exactly to Fix a Sluggish iPad

Is your iPad working slowly? Might it get bogged down after a couple of hours? At the same time as this is extra, not uncommon with old iPads that don't have the control power of the new iPad Air and iPad Pro Tablets, even the latest iPad can impede. A couple of multiple reasons just why an iPad could also begin operating slow, such as an application having troubles or a sluggish web connection. Thankfully, that is generally easy to revive.

- **First: stop all of your new apps**

One common reason behind an iPad to start chugging is a problem with the application itself instead of the iPad. If you enjoy a form that is working slower than usual, it could sound reasonable to go through the home button to close the application and re-launch it. However, pressing the home button wouldn't normally close out the app. It suspends the app, which mostly keeps it freezing in the backdground.

Some applications even continue steadily to run in the backdrop mode. Those are usually applications that stream music like Pandora, Spotify, or the melody app that is included with the iPad.

If the hassle is specifically with an individual app, we'll need to stop from it using the duty display. This may correctly close the application down and purge it from memory space, permitting you to release a 'fresh' version from it. Please discover that you might lose unsaved functions by exiting the app. If it's currently working on an objective, it could be better to make the application finishes the duty before proceeding.

Within the job screen, it is an excellent concept to have a summary of any applications that are taking part in music. It's not likely they may be causing a headache, or even if the application is loading the track from the web, it will not expend enough of your bandwidth to rely upon. However, last from the app won't hurt, and maybe sure the application isn't impacting something.

To shut the program, you will need to constitute a summary of all apps that will be operating in the background.

- **Double-click the home button in the bottom of your iPad**.

When you press it two times in quick succession, your most up to date applications are shown as cascading home windows across the screen. You might navigate via this screen by swiping from left-to-right or right-to-left.

The windows can have a related application icon above it.

***To close an app:

- Keep the finger down at the home display window.

- Without lifting your finger from the screen, swipe in the direction of the very best of the screen.

***This gesture resembles "*flicking*" the application from the iPad. Remember: you Tap the application windowpane, not the application icon.

Reboot the iPad

Closing the applications may not continuously do just fine. Within this example, rebooting the iPad is the product quality recourse. This will flush from memory and offer your iPad a fresh start.

NB: many humans believe the iPad forces down as the rest/wake button on the top right-hand corner of the iPad is pressed down or as the flap of their smart cover or bright case is closed, but this places the iPad in droop/suspend setting.

To reboot the iPad:

- Keep down the rest/wake button until instructions appear; letting you know to glide a button to power from the iPad.

- When you slip the button, the tablet will turn off, and the iPad's screen should go dark.

Wait around several seconds and then start the iPad up pressing down the rest/wake button once again. You'll first start to see the Apple brand logo design on the screen as well as your iPad need. Your iPad must run extra fast but, if it begins bogging down, retain in mind the apps that are running at that time. Once in a while, a single application can purpose the iPad to execute poorly.

Is your iPad still walking slower than you want?

Check your wireless connection

It could not be your iPad that is working sluggishly. It could be your mobile network.

You can attempt the internet speed of your Wi-Fi network by using an application like ***Ookla's Speedtest***. This application will send information to a remote server and then dispatches records back to the iPad, looking into each send and download rates of speed.

The usual Wi-Fi network in the U.S. Gets around 12 megabits-per-second (Mbps), though it is unusual to see rates of speed of 25+ Mbps. You possibly might not see plenty of the slowdown using your connection until it receives around 6 Mbps or significantly less. It is across the amount of bandwidth it requires to stream films and video.

If you're experiencing a headache with your Wi-Fi connection, try moving nearer to your router. If the pace increases, you might look at improving your Wi-Fi range. That's common in more prominent structures, but even a little home could have troubles.

Ensure you're updated to the latest version of iOS

iOS is the operating device working on the iPad. At precisely the same time as the best revise sometimes will positively sluggish the iPad down a little, it's always a great idea to perform the latest operating-system on device. Not handiest will this make sure that you have the most up to date efficiency tweaks, it additionally warranties you have present fixes for just about any protection problems.

Setup an ad-blocker

If you're mainly seeing a decline when surfing the internet in the safari internet browser, however, your web velocity is not sluggish, with the ability to be more an indicator of which webpages you're surfing than the iPad itself.

The more significant advertisements with a web page, the much longer it does take to load. Moreover, if some of those advertisements stall out, you might be left anticipating the web page to pop-up.

One fashion to this is to set up an advertisement blocker. Those widgets beautify the safari web browser by using disallowing advertisements to weight on the internet website. They make each for more straightforward reading and faster launching. Sites such as this one generate income from adverts, which means this is a balance you have to fight.

Flip off background app refresh

Background app refresh let applications to refresh their content even when you are not utilizing them. In this manner, Facebook might Tap base and retrieve articles in your post wall, or an information app may also fetch the newest articles.

However, this runs on your processing rate and your web connection, so that it can make the iPad to perform just a little slower. This usually isn't the theory cause, but if you frequently find the iPad working slow (and if the electric battery drains quickly), you must flip off background app refresh.

Showing off background application refresh:

- Head to your iPad's configurations.

- Choose **General** from the left-hand navigation menu.

- Tap the background application refresh.

- Tap the on/off slider near the top of the screen.

If you are nevertheless experiencing progressive speeds, there is certainly yet another factor you can do.

Clear STORAGE SPACE

If you're operating desperately low on space for storage, clearing up a little more room for the iPad can on occasion, improve efficiency. This will be achieved by deleting applications that you haven't used for quite a long time, particularly video games you don't play anymore.

It's clean to see which applications are employing the most space on your iPad:

1.	Head to **Settings.**

2.	Select **General** from the left-hand navigation menu.

3.   Tap **storage space & iCloud usage**.

4.   Tap **Manage Storage Space** (under the very best storage program). This may demonstrate which apps are using up the utmost storage.

You can additionally increase safari when you delete your cookies and internet background, although this might purpose you to log back to any websites that have saved your login records.

CHAPTER 12

How to Extend iPad's Battery Strength

With every iPad release, one continuous point remains. The iPad is now faster, and the images get better every year. Nevertheless, the device works with the first 10 hours of battery life. However, also for those individuals that use their iPad 24hrs each day, it's still easy for it to perform. Moreover, there is nothing worse than looking to stream video from Netflix and then have that low battery message pop-up and interrupt your show.

Thankfully, there are a few tips you could utilize to keep iPad battery life and hold that from happening as often. Concealed secrets that will change you into an iPad expert:

Right here's how you can get the best of your iPad's battery life span:

- **Adjust the brightness:** The iPad comes with an automatic-brightness feature which facilitates the iPad predicated on the light quality within the area, but this program isn't always enough. Modifying the overall lighting could be the first solitary thing you can do to help ease out a little more from your battery consumption. You can transform the light by starting the iPad's configurations, choosing screen & view from the left-side menu and moving the brightness slider. The goal is to get it to a stage where it's nevertheless comfortable enough to learn, however nearly as shiny as the default establishing.

- **Switch off Bluetooth:** Most of us haven't any Bluetooth devices linked to the iPad, so all the Bluetooth carrier does for all of us is waste charge of the iPad's battery life. When you have no Bluetooth devices connected, ensure Bluetooth is switched off. A brief way to turn the transfer for Bluetooth off is to open up the iPad manager - panel by swiping up from the backside of the screen.

- **Switch off Location services:** At precisely the same time as even the Wi-Fi version of the iPad will do a fantastic job of identifying its location, most people do not use the location service on our iPad as much as we utilize them on our iPad. Turning OFF GPS is a concise and clean manner to save lots of a little battery even while not quitting any feature. Also, remember if you need to use GPS, you may switch it **ON**. You can switch off location services in the iPad's configurations below privacy.

- **Turn off notification:** While notification is an excellent feature, it can drain a small amount of battery life because the tool assessments to check on if it needs to force a notification to the screen. If you want to do the most to optimize your battery life, you can turn drive notification off completely. You could likewise turn it off for specific apps, reducing all of the push notifications you obtain. You may switch off notification in configurations.

- **Fetch email less regularly:** With default configurations, the iPad will check out brand spanking new email each quarter-hour. Pushing this back to a half-hour or one hour can help your battery last much longer. Move to configurations, choose the email settings and select the "fetch new data" choice. This will enable you to set how often your iPad fetches email. There could even be a choice only to have check email manually.

- **Switch off 4G:** More often than not, we use the iPad at home, this means the use from it via our mobile data connection on. We utilize it at home exclusively. If you regularly end up low on battery, a good suggestion is to turn off your 4G data connection. This may protect it from draining any power when you are not using it.

- **Turn off background application refresh:** Background app refresh keeps your apps up to date by relaxing them even while the iPad is idle or as long as you're on various other apps. This may drain a little extra battery strength. Get into configurations, choose General configurations and scroll down till you find "background app refresh." You can choose to turn off the service or certainly flip off specific apps you don't want to run in the background.

- **Discover apps consuming your battery:** Do you realize you could test thoroughly your iPad's battery usage? That is a fantastic manner to find what applications you're using the most and which apps can be consuming more than their expected percentage of your battery. You could test utilization within the iPad's configurations by choosing battery from the left-hand side menu.

- **Match iPad improvements:** It's continuously important to keep iOS updated to the latest from

Apple. Not merely would this help optimize the battery life of the iPad, it also ensures you're getting the latest security fix and patching any bugs that have popped up, which allows the iPad run efficiently.

- **Reduce Animation:** That is a technique to save a little of battery life and make the iPad show up a bit more reactive. The iPad's user interface consists of a few animations like glass windows zooming in and zooming out, and the parallax influence on icons, which makes them seem to hover over the backdrop picture. You can turn off those user interface effect by heading to **Settings**, Tapping **General Settings**, Tap **Display,** and getting to reduce animation to get it turned **Off**.

- **Buy a Smart Case:** The smart case can save battery life by placing the iPad into **Sleep mode** when you close the flap. It might not look like a great deal of conservation, however in case you aren't with the habit of striking the rest/wake button each time you have completed using the iPad; it could help offer you a supplementary five, ten or even quarter-hour extension of battery strength by the end of the day.

CHAPTER 13

How to Fix iPad that won't Charge

If you're having troubles charging your iPad when it's linked to your personal computer, you are in good company. While your iPad or iPod device might not have a difficulty charging when connected to the USB slot on your pc, the iPad requires substantially higher power. This means that some USB slots, especially the ones on old computer systems, genuinely don't have the feature to get the duty performed.

How to see whether your iPad is charging

If the device has enough power to charge the iPad, a lightning bolt can be shown within the center of the battery meter at the very top right-hand corner of the iPad.

If it generally does not have enough capacity to charge the iPad, you might start to see the phrases "not charging" next to the battery meter.

Usually, the iPad can be charged using the computer if you positioned it in active mode. However, if the computer is set into sleep mode, the iPad will not charge.

The smooth and straightforward answer is to plug the iPad into a power outlet by using the adapter that is included with the iPad. That's also the quickest way to charge the iPad. Even personal computers that could effectively charge the iPad may not place out almost as much current as a standard charger. Some power strips additionally have USB ports to charge USB devices, which may be an incredible manner to charge the iPad.

Trouble charging the iPad when Connected to Power Outlet

First, be sure the iPad does not have a software problem by rebooting it. To achieve that, press down the sleep button on the top right-hand corner of the iPad. After some mere seconds, a crimson button can appear instructing you to slip it to the power of these devices.

Allow it shut down completely, and then click the power button down to power ON. You might start to see the apple brand logo appear at the center of the screen even while it boots up.

If the iPad still doesn't charge using the electrical outlet, you may have to check your cable or the adapter. You could discover if you have trouble with the cable by linking the iPad to your laptop with the cable.

If you start to see the lightning bolt on battery meter or

"not charging" next to the battery meter, you know the wire is working. If this is the case, absolutely buy a new adapter.

If the computer will not respond when you plug in the iPad, it is then not recognizing the iPad connected, meaning the issue is possibly with the cable.

In rare circumstances, while changing the adapter and the cable will not do just fine, you might have a hardware issue with the iPad. If so, you'll need to contact Apple for support. (If you live near an Apple Store, try getting in touch with the customer support. Apple Store staff can be quite accommodating.)